Commie Currency

Commie Currency
The abuse of money in the Soviet Union

Timothy E. Buchanan

EAGLE MOUNTAIN PRESS

MMXI

Copyright © 2011 by Timothy E. Buchanan

timothybuchanan.org

All Rights Reserved

ISBN 978-0-9831749-1-2
LCCN 2011922837

For my wife—

who gave me her Russian money (worthless)

and her Russian soul (priceless).

Contents

Foreword: Money is Theft ... 1

One: Traditional and Provisional
END OF THE OLD REGIME ... 5
PROVISIONALLY SPEAKING ... 9
PLATES ... 13

Two: War Communism
A PLETHORA OF SYMBOLS ... 21
A TOKEN OF MY ACCOUNTING ... 22
THE TOWER OF BABBLE ... 23
TWO STEPS FORWARD, ONE STEP BACK ... 25
PLATES ... 29

Three: White Guard, Red Blood
EASTERN DRIVE ... 37
THE FAR FROM QUIET DON ... 39
BALTIC SIDESHOW ... 40
I AM THE WALRUS ... 42
THE HOUSE OF SPECIAL PURPOSE ... 44
BEYOND THE CAUCASUS ... 45
THE GEORGIAN AND THE GEORGIAN QUESTION ... 47
PLATES ... 49

Four: Main Enemy
TALE OF TWO CITIES ... 59
ON THE BLEEDING EDGE ... 60
SIBERIAN CIRCUS ... 63
ONE AND UNDIVIDED ... 67
PLATES ... 71

Five: Promises, Promises

DEAD FIVER	83
GIVE ME LIBERTY (AND RUBLES)	84
WAR CREDIT	85
ADOPT A BOND	86
PLATES	89

Six: Hyper, Bipaper, and Union

PURGING ZEROS	93
CHERVONETS	94
THE AGONY OF THE ZNAKI	95
CRISIS AND REFORM	97
PLATES	99

Seven: Stability, Suppression, and Stasis

TASTE OF THERMIDOR AND THE QUINQUENNIUM	105
THE GREAT TERRORIST	107
PATRIOTIC WAR, PAPER REFORM	109
THE LONG GOODBYE	111
PLATES	115

Eight: Had a Great Fall

THE REFORMER UNRAVELS THE SYSTEM	125
REPEATEDLY BITTEN, FINALLY SHY	128
THE PROBLEM OF PRIVATIZATION	129
MMM: A CLASSIC PYRAMID	130
PLATES	133

Afterword: Money is Information

	141

Foreword: Money is Theft

The liveliest streets of London are crowded with stores whose show windows are filled with the riches of the world, Indian shawls, American revolvers, Chinese porcelain, Parisian corsets, Russian furs and tropical spices, but all of these things of joy bear fatal white labels with Arabic figures with the laconic characters £ s. d. Such is the picture of the commodity in circulation.[1]

This passage, from Karl Marx's *Critique of Political Economy,* is both amusing and instructive. It is amusing for its clichés—American revolvers counterpoised with Parisian corsets—and instructive for Marx's low esteem of those odious labels, with their plainly marked, and somehow disturbing, prices. But why did Marx so despise money?

The following explanation of Marxist attitudes towards money is adapted from chapters I through IX of *Capital,* a philosophical text so turgid and opaque[2] that few readers make it past the first volume.[3] Marx himself failed to finish volume three, instead depositing the manuscript on his shelf—there to languish for ten years until his death.[4] The core of Marxism, however, can be reduced to a few simple propositions and arguments.

Begin with the commodity: "a thing that by its properties satisfies human wants of some sort or another." Whatever want our thing satisfies defines its *use-value;* for example, an apple's use-value is to be eaten. Instead of being consumed, commodities may be traded; for example, I may have a surfeit of apples and desire to trade some for firewood, to stay warm. The quantity of apples I must trade to get firewood tells us its *exchange-value*. Marx concerns himself with exchange-values, finding little of interest in the fact that all commodities are, in the end, consumed.

A commodity's exchange-value is, Marx argues, determined by the amount of human labor that went into its preparation: gathering apples or chopping firewood. Therefore, we *need* a commodity for its utility, but we *value* it according to what we may get for it. Thus, Marx says, we make a *fetish* of the commodity. Moreover, exchange-value disguises the fact that we are actually exchanging labor for labor, hidden in the exchange of commodity for commodity. In short, it is all about labor, with Marx.

Subdivision of labor made exchange of commodities necessary (before that, each family produced all their needs), and necessitated also a medium to facilitate the process of exchange and to quantify exchange values. Here, money

---

1   Karl Marx, Contribution to a Critique of Political Economy (New York: Charles H. Kerr, 1904), 108.

2   Marx's writing style has been aptly depicted as "verbal constipation coupled with a bad case of hemorrhoids." Gary North, "The Marx Nobody Knows," in *Requiem for Marx,* ed. Yuri N. Maltsev (Auburn, AL: Ludwig von Mises Institute, 1993), 86.

3   Karl Marx, *Capital: a Critique of Political Economy,* vol. 1, *The Process of Capitalist Production,* ed. Frederick Engels, trans. Samuel Moore and Edward Aveling (New York: International Publishers, 1967), 35-217.

4   In the final chapter, Marx promises to give a definition of the term *class,* then abandons the effort. One might think that in a work about class conflict, this should have been handled at the beginning. Engels gives a misleading impression by adding "Here the manuscript breaks off," as if death had taken Marx at his writing desk.

Commie Currency

enters the picture. Marx identifies two types of exchange processes in which money serves very different purposes.

In the first, a commodity is exchanged for money that is then exchanged for another commodity, C-M-C in Marx's terminology. The money expresses the equal exchange-value of the two commodities, and merely represents a lengthening of direct exchange, C-C. If I sell my apples and buy an equal value of firewood, then no one has lost or gained. However, money also gives rise to another, for Marx, more insidious process of exchange, M-C-M. Here, a person begins with money, uses it to buy a commodity, and then sells it to receive money back again. Why is this bad?

Money is unique among commodities in that it is wanted, not for its use-value, but for its exchange-value. C-M-C reduces to C-C and two participants who each receive something they can use, but M-C-M reduces to M-M and one person—who will not be satisfied with receiving back exactly what he had before. He desires, somehow, to increase the exchange-value of the commodity and thereby receive an increase in money. What is the source of this *surplus-value*?

Once again, it is labor. Here, Marx makes the not unreasonable assumption that the exchange-value of the products that a factory worker may make in a day is greater than the cost of the materials needed to sustain that worker: food, shelter, clothing. The person who purchases the labor, the factory owner, keeps this extra value and so receives back more money than he spent in building the factory, buying the materials, and paying the worker.

To summarize: money, an inevitable development of exchange, itself an inevitable product of the subdivision of labor, is neutral when it is used to facilitate the exchange of commodities wanted for their utility. But money may also be turned into capital, enabling the money-holder, now a capitalist, to expropriate the value imparted by the labor of his workers to the products they create, but he owns. For Marx, the increase of money is the root of all evil.

But Marx's scheme depends on the absolute equality of all trades. Surely, no one would bother to make an exchange unless he believed himself to be better off as a result.[5] The market exists because it does tend to make parties better off. The nature of exchange is not equality but *double-inequality,* and that makes malarkey of Marx's mathematics.[6]

Marx's downtrodden workers (he used cotton spinners as example) were able to produce surplus-value only by virtue of the expensive capital investments that they used. But for Marx, unskilled labor was all, and he derides the contribution of the capitalist investor. In his cotton factory tale, for example, Marx has the supervisor and manager "try to hide their smiles" when the owner claims his own work has value. But in Marx's tale, the owner laughs all the way to the bank, for the "workman creates surplus value which, for the capitalist, has all the charms of a creation out of nothing."

For Marx, money was the manifestation of humanity's alienation from labor and the *sine qua non* of inhumane exploitation. Capitalism, the economic system that Marx despised, is possible only when persons save (or as he puts it, hoard) money, using their savings to purchase machinery, materials, and labor—and thereby produce profit.

---

5 Marxists would sniff that this is an example of "false consciousness."

6 Murray N. Rothbard, *Man, Economy, and State* (Auburn, AL: Ludwig von Mises Institute, 2009), 103.

Foreword: Money is Theft

Marx's loathing of money is obvious in the passage quoted above, and elsewhere in his writings. For example, in "The Power of Money," Marx laments that money enables the most ugly of men to buy "the most beautiful of women," enabling the possessor of money to be "capable of all that the human heart longs for."[7]

Elsewhere, Marx claimed "Money is not a thing; it is a social relation."[8] Marx hated the relationships that currency made possible. He dreamed of the day when money would be abolished, and each person would receive all things "according to his needs."[9]

Marx's Russian disciples longed for the post-money millennium. The Bolsheviks' chief theoreticians described their vision of utopia, in a primer for acolytes:

> The Communist mode of production, therefore, is not production for the market, but for the needs of the community.... These goods are not exchanged against one another; they are neither bought nor sold. They are simply taken to the communal stores, and there given to whomever requires them. Under this system money is not necessary.[10]

For Marxists, money is both the alpha and the omega of capitalism. It is simultaneously the means of acquiring capital, by which exploitation of the worker is possible, and the reward from this process of theft.

How then would Marx's followers behave, once they got their hands on an actual economy, and its money supply? We have an example for study: an entire life cycle of a Marxist nation, from its violent birth in 1917 to farcical death in 1991. The history of currency in the Soviet Union is the subject of this study: *Commie Currency*.

MAY DAY, 2011

---

7   Karl Marx, *Economic and Philosophic Manuscripts*, trans. Martin Milligan (New York: International Publishers, 1964), 167.

8   Karl Marx, *The Poverty of Philosophy* (Moscow: Co-Operative Publishing Society, 1935), 68.

9   His own needs must have been very great, because Marx spent several fortunes (not his) in his lifetime. See North, 75-105.

10   N. Bucharin and Preobraschensky, *ABC of Communism*, translated from a German version by P. Lavin (Calcutta, India: Century Press, 1952), 62.

One: Traditional and Provisional

It has been said that if Nicholas II, the last tsar, had been more intelligent, then there would have been no Kerensky; if the Prime Minister of the Provisional Government had been smarter, then there would have been no Lenin.[1] It is true that both Nicholas and Kerensky acted in ways that, in retrospect, seem intended to turn them out of office. Nicholas, for his part, suffered from ambivalence; court wags jested that the most powerful man in Russia was whoever had last spoken to the tsar. Kerensky, as we shall see, had quite the opposite problem. In contrast to the tsar of imperial Russia, imperial currency was stable and dependable, thanks to its backing.

END OF THE OLD REGIME

The excellence of the gold standard is to be seen in the fact that it renders the determination of the monetary unit's purchasing power independent of the policies of governments and political parties.[2]

Under the gold standard, a government guarantees that its currency can be exchanged for a fixed amount of specie (gold coin valued by weight) and, consequently, that the exchange rate is fixed in respect to other participating nations. During its heyday, 1880-1914, the gold standard held price inflation to nearly nothing, a source of confidence for investors. Its attraction for a developing country such as Russia was that gold convertibility reassured foreigners, who funded much-needed capital improvements.

Imperial Russia joined the gold standard after more than a century of failed fiat money. Her first currency, issued from 1769, was the *assignat,* a term more commonly associated with the French Revolution. Assignats circulated alongside specie, but depreciated deeply against coinage due to over issue, especially during the Napoleonic War.

Assignats were replaced in 1841 with *State Credit Notes,* redeemable in silver rubles, but these were also debased by over abundance. For example, during the Crimean War (1853-1856), the amount in paper rubles in circulation more than doubled, from 311 million to 735 million; subsequently, redemption in specie was suspended.[3]

To reform the credit note, the State Bank was formed in 1860, but made little progress until the 1890s, when Minister of Finance S.Y. Witte ended free coinage of silver and placed the paper ruble on the gold standard. The Monetary Reform of 1897 allowed issuance of 600 million paper rubles on a fifty percent gold reserve, with full backing required above that amount.[4] From then until the outbreak of the Great War, Russia enjoyed economic growth, if not political stability.

Our first example of Tsarist currency is a ten-ruble note from 1909.[5] This particular bill was found in a shop in Jaffa, Israel, where once, probably, a Russian pilgrim to the Holy Land

---

1   One might extend the analogy to Lenin and Stalin.
2   Ludwig von Mises, *The Theory of Money And Credit* (Auburn, Alabama: Ludwig von Mises Institute, 2009), 416.

---

3   *Ministry of Finance, 1802-1902* (St. Petersburg, 1902) in Arthur Arnold, *Banks, Credit, and Money in Soviet Russia* (New York: Columbia University Press, 1937), 5.
4   Arnold, 13-14.
5   Currency and bonds are reproduced at the end of each chapter, and, except where noted, are full-size.

Commie Currency

used it to buy supplies.[6] These notes were widely accepted, thanks to their gold backing and to printing techniques developed in St. Petersburg.

In the 1890s, Ivan Orlov, an engineer at the imperial currency plant, developed a new machine to print multicolored patterns in one pass. The *Orlovskaya Pechat,* the Orlov Stamp, produced bills that were " splendid in artistic respects" and, more importantly, were difficult to counterfeit.[7] Orlov's technique, which permitted perfect alignment of diversely colored typography and backgrounds, won for him an award of 7000 rubles from the tsar.

The rate of exchange into gold is prominent on the obverse of these bills, above the signatures of the printing plant manager and the state cashier:

> The State Bank will exchange credit notes for gold money in unrestricted amounts. (1 Ruble = 1/15 Imperial, and consists of 17.424 dolia of pure gold).

17.424 dolia was equal to 11.94792 grains[8]; therefore, a ten-ruble note could be exchanged for almost one-quarter troy ounce of gold.[9] In 1914, however, the State Bank suspended the payment of specie—as did the other belligerents in the Great War. No Russian government since then has backed its money with anything more than promises, in spite of what we will read on some of their bills.

Largely due to dependable money, Russia was having an economic boom before disaster struck. "By 1913, her gross industrial output was 219% higher than in 1900."[10] The State Bank held 1.5 billion rubles in gold reserves to back 1.6 billion in paper, far more than required by law.[11] Upon a background of increasing prosperity, with rubles backed by gold and a high demand for Imperial bonds, Nicholas II celebrated 300 years of Romanov rule. Living in exile in Zurich, Lenin despaired of achieving revolution, lamenting "Why not three hundred more?"

The Tercentennial of 1913 is the gauge by which we measure the ensuing catastrophes of war, civil war, and the Communist regime. Curiously, Soviet economists also employed 1913 as their yardstick, as they devised their planned economy. Commenting on the results, a post-Soviet photographic narrative noted: "Grain production per head of population did not reach 1913 levels again until the mid-1960s."[12]

What were workers paid in 1913? A survey of workers in the Moscow garment industry found that skilled tailors earned 37 rubles per month, while subcontracted workers were paid 23.[13] Apparently, out-sourcing was popular even then. "The elite in machine tool plants could make 40

---

6 Jaffa was the port of arrival for the many Orthodox *palomniki,* pilgrims. For a moving account by a British writer who passed as a Russian pilgrim, see Stephen Graham, *With the Russian Pilgrims to Jerusalem* (annotated edition forthcoming from Eagle Mountain Press).

7 A. Michaelis and L. Kharlamov, *Paper Money of Russia* (Perm, Russia: Goznak Press, 1993), 17. (All translations from Russian are mine unless indicated otherwise.)

8 Arnold, 14.

9 Worth almost $350 in mid-December 2010.

10 Michael Kettle, *The Allies and the Russian Collapse* (New York: Harper & Collins, 1981), 21.

11 Arnold, 15.

12 Brian Moynahan, *The Russian Century: a photographic history of Russia's 100 years* (New York: Random House, 1994), 36.

13 E. A. Oliunina, " The Tailoring Trade in Moscow," in Victoria Bonnell ed., *The Russian Worker* (Berkeley: University of California Press, 1983), 167.

One: Traditional and Provisional

to 50 rubles,"[14] but most factory workers earned less. Female sales clerks received pitiful wages, typically five to twenty rubles a month, while the "highest salaries were paid to the directors, solicitors, and business managers of commercial firms."[15] These CEOs of their time earned 6,000 to 10,000 rubles a year, but our ten-ruble note would have been a week's pay for a skilled factory worker.

What did things cost? Everyone in the working-class family that could work, would work: husband, wife, children barely in their teens. Together, they might bring in 50 to 100 rubles each month, spending 20-30% of that for lodging, 40-50% for food, and 5-10% for alcohol. Many people lived and ate in facilities supplied by their employers, supplied at lower rates but at commensurately lower quality. Employer-supplied housing and cafeterias formed a pattern that was followed by the Soviets.

On the New York Exchange in 1913, two rubles were worth approximately one dollar, where gold was pegged at $20.67. Russian workers earned far less than Americans, but their wages were beginning to approach those in parts of Western Europe. The ruble was, before the war that destroyed the dynasty and the party that sacked the economy, a hard currency, the lifeblood of a vibrant developing economy.

Our next example is a 25-ruble credit note, also from 1909, but oriented horizontally. This format is more usual for Russian money, but authorities sometimes used an attention-getting vertical form when a monetary change was implemented. In other words, re-form could indicate reform, a gimmick also employed by the Soviets.

Depicted on this note is Tsar Alexander III, a conservative, even repressive, ruler who developed the *Okhrana,* the secret police and forerunner to Lenin's *Cheka.* He also re-established State control of universities, and tightened censorship rules. Alexander's distaste for radicals and intellectuals is understandable, however. Revolutionaries had killed his father, the liberal Alexander II, in 1881, literally blowing him to pieces for his efforts at reform.[16] As befitting a ruler obsessed with control, the rules governing the currency are printed next to Alexander III's portrait:

> 1. Exchange of State Credit Notes for gold money is insured by all government property.
> 2. State Credit Notes circulate throughout the Empire at par with gold money.
> 3. Those guilty of counterfeiting Credit Notes are subject to forfeiture of all civil rights and exile at hard labor.

Alexander's portrait illustrates why his family called him the "Bull." His strength was such that Alexander would often amuse people by bending a silver ruble (think of an old-fashioned silver dollar, but thicker) around one of his fingers.

Ironically, his great strength led to Alexander's early death. When the imperial train derailed at Borki in October 1888, the tsar held the collapsed roof of the saloon car on his back until

---

14   Moynahan, 34.
15   A. M. Gudvan, "Essays on the History of the Movement of Sales-Clerical Workers in Russia," in *The Russian Worker,* 202.

16   At the time of his murder, the tsar had, in his pocket, a draft version of a proposed constitutional government. His assassins—"People's Will," they called themselves—wanted to stymie moderation and thereby encourage radicalization; at this they succeeded.

Commie Currency

his family escaped. Subsequent medical problems led to his early death in 1894, a few months shy of his fiftieth birthday, and the accession of his hapless heir, Nicholas.

There was nothing hapless about Peter the Great, who is pictured on the next, massive bill, the largest—in size and denomination—that the Tsarist government ever issued.[17] Goznak (the Soviet mint) later judged this bill to be "the peak of creativity of the workers in the Design Department for State Paper."[18]

The portrait of Peter was taken from the painting by Jean-Marc Nattier that hangs in the Hermitage, which illustrated his love for the West. At his court, nobles were forced to wear western garb; Russian men had to cut their beloved beards or pay a tax to keep them.

Another, less formal portrait of Peter was used in a watermark on the right. This provided an additional security measure for this large bill, worth nearly twelve-and-a-half ounces of gold.[19]

The female figure is an allegorical Mother Russia; she holds laurel leaves representing honor, a shield standing for might, and a scepter topped with the Romanov eagle. Classical references abound on this bill, from the columns topped with cupids to the crown and orb placed above and below Peter (the world at his feet!). Classical allegory was popular in the late empire, and continued to be used on currency printed by the Whites during the Civil War.

When this bill was printed, in 1912 or 1913 at the height of the boom, 500 rubles was a month's salary for an upper-level manager, a year's wages to a worker. Then came the Great War.

There are three ways for a government to fund a war: raising taxes, borrowing, and printing. In Tsarist Russia, the largest single source of revenue came from the liquor tax—one reason workers spent ten percent of their income on that palliative.[20] That source could hardly be tapped further, especially as the government hoped to curtail military inebriation. Nor could the government borrow what was needed. Many state bonds had been sold to foreigners, who now had to fund their own adventures; moreover, Germans had been among the largest investors.

The printing presses, however, were in good order, and by the end of 1915, the quantity of paper rubles in circulation had tripled. Prices rose by 30% that year, while wage increases were less than half of that. Obedient to Gresham's Law that bad money drives out good money, silver coinage disappeared, as gold had vanished in 1914. A substitute for small change had to be devised.

During the happier days of the Tercentennial, the Russian postal service issued stamps honoring the tsars; Nicholas II was featured on these ten-kopeck stamps. They were not widely used, however, because postal clerks often refused to 'deface' the tsar with cancellation marks.

In 1915 another use was found for the stamps and they were issued as small change. Instead of adhesive, the reverse bore an admonishment: "placed in circulation on an equal basis with silver money." Of course, no one in his right mind

---

17 This bill has been reduced by 25%.

18 A. Michaelis and L. Kharlamov, unpaginated illustration.

19 The watermark has been digitally enhanced to make it visible.

20 In America also, liquor funded the Federal Government, providing as much as 40% of revenue in some years. Prohibitionists pressed for passage of the income tax amendment, as a necessary precursor for an amendment to outlaw the sale of alcohol.

One: Traditional and Provisional

would have exchanged silver for these scraps, and coins remained hidden in hoards.

The stamps ranged in value from one to twenty kopecks, and half-ruble tokens, such as this one, were issued to fill the gap between stamps and credit bills. The 50-kopeck tokens were cheaply printed, *sans* signatures or serial numbers.

Both stamps and tokens were issued again in 1917 by the Provisional government, but without the Romanov eagle, and stating that they replaced all "metal money." By then, even copper had disappeared from circulation. The stamp bearing Nicholas II was not included in the second issue; perhaps it was considered bad taste.

Prices continued to rise throughout 1915 and 1916 as the war demanded more resources. Ironically, it was the monarchy's attempt to economize that finally brought down the régime. Tens of thousands of new recruits were needed each week, to feed the hungry maw of the Eastern Front. Fresh from the villages of rural Russia, these draftees were garrisoned in the capital so as to centralize training and thereby reduce costs. Conditions at the camp were brutal, with 160,000 men crammed into barracks meant for 20,000. Facing a bleak future in the trenches, these raw recruits became easy targets for the Socialist agitators.

> In view of the fact that the February Revolution is often depicted as a worker revolt, it is important to emphasize that it was, first and foremost, a mutiny of peasant soldiers whom, *to save money,* the authorities had billeted in overcrowded facilities in the empire's capital city—in the words of one eyewitness, like "kindling wood near a powder keg."[21]

Our final imperial state credit note is a one-ruble bill. Although it is dated 1898, we know from the signatures and the serial number that it was printed in 1915. Many identically numbered bills were issued at this time, each beginning with the letters NV (НВ in Cyrillic). A paragraph on the note claims that it may be exchanged for gold, at the rate set 18 years earlier, but that is untrue.

The monogram of Nicholas II is contained within the circle on the right side, with the Romanov eagle on the left. Since this was the last currency issued by the Romanovs, the bill's (unintentional) resemblance to a sepulcher is appropriate.

PROVISIONALLY SPEAKING

Shielded by his advisors, Nicholas had no way of knowing the actual situation in his capital in February 1917 and ordered a crackdown. Instead, the soldiers joined with the demonstrators. Now abandoned by his military, the tsar abdicated.

At that point, Russian politics became a struggle between the *Soviets* (ad hoc socialist councils) and the *Duma,* the more-or-less elected parliament that Nicholas had tolerated since the failed 1905 Revolution. The Duma had greater political legitimacy, but was constrained in action by *Order Nº 1,* which required all decisions of the Duma to be submitted for approval by the Petrograd Soviet. For the next eight months, therefore, Russia was run by *diarchy,* a dual-government that was inherently unstable.

---

21 Richard Pipes, *The Russian Revolution* (New York: Random House, 1991), 278. Emphasis added.

Commie Currency

Nicholas II signed the abdication on 2 March 1917, and the unusual government that took power began to issue new currency almost immediately. Later that month, the Commissar of Artistic Matters for the Executive Soviet of Workers and Soldiers (there may have been some euphonious acronym for this office) sent his suggestions to the Minister of Finance of the Provisional government. Designers and printers moved quickly and, on 26 April, a new State Credit Bill was issued.

The Tsarist government had been turning out reams of paper rubles to pay for the war. The volume of currency in circulation had increased nearly seven-fold since July 1914, and the price index in April 1917 was 3.35.[22] The largest Tsarist denomination was 500 rubles; the Provisionals decided to double that. Thus was set in motion a process of denominational inflation.

The designers and printers were justly pleased with this 1000-ruble creation.[23] The Orlov Stamp was used with four colors. The obverse carried the usual claim that it could be exchanged for gold, but the reverse, shown here, posed a puzzle for the designers. The new administration had, as yet, no symbols, but some kind of representation of the government was wanted to ensure the new note's acceptance.

Since 1906 the Tauride Palace had been used by the Duma, and the Petrograd Soviet ensconced itself there during the February Revolution. This building was depicted on the new currency, basking in the sunlight to show that enlightenment had come to Russia.

The reality inside the Tauride was far different. Because of monarchial maneuvers, the Duma was hardly a representative body, while the Executive Soviet of Workers and Soldiers had not a single factory worker as a delegate. In fact, unruly servicemen made up two-thirds of the Soviet.

Lenin had just returned to Russia, on a train thoughtfully provided by the German government, but the Bolsheviks were a minority party in spite of their name (which means the majority). The Mensheviks (meaning, naturally, the minority) had three times as many seats on the Executive, the committee that steered the Soviet.

Alexander Kerensky had been elected vice-chairman of the Executive Soviet and was also a member of the Temporary Committee of the Duma. After the February Revolution, Kerensky ascended to the position of Minister of Justice in the new administration, then worked as Minister of War, and finally rose to become Prime Minister. He thought of himself as the man who would save Russia; instead, his blunder delivered the country to Lenin.

It all came back to the war, which had brought down the tsar and would, in turn, discredit the Provisional government. The carnage of that protracted conflict kept the military ranks in constant turmoil. After the February revolution, the Petrograd Garrison could only with difficulty be persuaded to return to their barracks.

Besides bodies, the war required money, lots of it. Tsarist notes of 100 and 500 rubles still circulated, along with what people were calling the *Dumki*. A proposal was made to fill the gap between the 100 and 500 denominations by simply slicing some Dumki into quarters, but that would have lowered the credibility of the administration still further and the idea was dropped.

On the heels of military setbacks in the summer of 1917, the money shortage became critical and a new note was released on 22 August.

---

22 Arnold, 49.

23 Image size reduced by 5%.

One: Traditional and Provisional

The 250-ruble bill used the same printing techniques, although the obverse was red, and the reverse, shown here, had the green background. The new ornamentation of this bill showed the paradigm shift in the Russian State, away from their Byzantine heritage.

After Constantinople fell to the Ottomans in 1453, the Muscovite rulers began to see themselves as proper heirs to that throne. Ivan III married the niece of the last Byzantine emperor and adopted the Greek double-headed eagle into the Russian imperial seal.[24] The Romanov eagle clutched the orb and scepter of imperial rule and displayed the seals of the cities of Rus.[25] Moscow itself was held to be the "Third Rome," the final repository of Christian Empire before the end times. In 1520, monk Filofei wrote to Vasily III to "take heed… two Romes have fallen, the third stands, and a fourth there shall not be."[26]

Post-monarchy, that heritage was to be swept away, or at least adapted to the tenor of the times. A new eagle was designed—lacking regal paraphernalia and with wings lowered—by an artist named Ivan Bilibin. He is best remembered for his theatrical designs and for illustrating children's books of Slavic myth and legend.

It is fitting that an artist who worked in fairy tales designed the coat-of-arms for what turned out to be an ephemeral administration. Looking beneath the wings-down eagle, however, we see an infamous symbol—what appears to be a Nazi swastika.

Swastika is Sanskrit, meaning "prosperity," and is an ancient symbol. In the early twentieth century, the symbol began to be associated with anti-Semitism. However, it is unlikely that such was the intent here, as the artist was himself Jewish. A description of the symbol was read aloud in the Duma on 6 June: "a geometric ornament formed of a cross-shape of intersecting broad lines (strips) turned at right angles."[27]

Other contemporary users of the swastika, such as the Finnish Air Force and the German *Freikorps*, drew the symbol with horizontal and vertical lines. Here, however, the swastika is turned on the diagonal, for that arrangement complements the lines of the eagle—head to tail and wing-to-wing. This composition predates Hitler's adoption of the diagonal swastika by some years; it is not known if he was aware of the prior use. It would be ironic indeed if Russia provided the core symbolism for her future deadly enemy.

The Nikolaevski, the Romanovski, and the Dumki could not fill the economic hole into which Russia was sliding. Kerensky had plans for a whole new series of notes, from one to 10,000 rubles, and had placed an order with the American Banknote Company. Delivery would take months, however, and Kerensky needed a stopgap measure.

State Bank director M. Shipov suggested that "blocks of consular stamps should be used for printing notes."[28] The resultant 20 and 40-ruble "Treasury Tokens" were printed on cheap stock, without signatures or serial numbers. People sniffed that such paper was fit "only to wrap

---

24 James H. Billington, *The Icon and the Axe* (New York: Vintage Books, 1970), 58.

25 One-ruble bill, page 19.

26 In *The Russian Chronicles* (San Diego: Thunder Bay Press, 2001), 100.

27 R.V. Nikolayev, *Money, Time, Power* (St. Petersburg: Petersburg Collector, 2002), 6.

28 Michael W. Bernatzky, "Monetary Policy," in *Russian Public Finance During the War* (New Haven, CT: Yale University Press, 1928), 387.

Commie Currency

sausage."[29] In a desperate attempt to win acceptance of the cheaply made currency, the administration appealed to the public:

> The Minister of Finance requests that no credence be given to those malicious persons who, having made their way into Russia from enemy countries… will be trying to promote a lack of confidence in the new bank notes.[30]

The phrase "malicious persons" may have been a jibe at Lenin and other Bolsheviks who had returned, with German assistance, to Russian soil. In any case, the appeal failed to convince the public and the tokens traded at a steep discount to tsarist currency. Moreover, the simple design made them easy to produce. Despite the warning printed on the bill's reverse, many counterfeits were printed. In fitting tribute to the hapless head of the Provisionals, the new tokens were known as *Kerenki*.

These particular Kerenki were found in an apartment that was being remodeled after the 1991 Soviet collapse, having been stashed there nearly eight decades earlier. Apparently, the owner either forgot where they were or did not bother to retrieve them. Incidentally, the fact that they remained hidden for so long indicates the degree of building maintenance in Soviet times.

Alexander Kerensky's government did not last as long as the tokens of his name. Convinced that the legitimacy of his administration lay in his commitment to the war (certainly, the Allies saw things that way), Kerensky agreed with new commander-in-chief Brusilov that a massive offensive was just the ticket. Russia sustained 400,000 dead and wounded in the failed "June Offensive." An even greater number deserted, swelling the growing ranks of the left.

Alarmed at the deterioration in discipline, Kerensky appointed a new C-in-C. General Lavr Kornilov was no monarchist, but he despised socialism, and soon came to loggerheads with the Provisional Government. Worried about a possible "Kornilov Revolt," the Prime Minister dismissed the popular general, placing him and thirty other officers under house arrest.

In fact, there was no plot, only rumors and provocations.[31] But a political aphorism of the time cautioned, "no enemies on the left." Seeing an imagined counter-revolution from the right, Kerensky broke faith with the military, and lost the trust of conservatives and moderates.

Kerensky attempted to rally support at a State Conference, held in Moscow in the middle of August. One glance at the delegates would expose the growing polarization of the country; the bankers and other conservatives sitting stolidly on the right, the soldiers moving restlessly in their seats to the left, and the Bolsheviks out on strike, making any reconciliation impossible. From August until October, the Provisional government was a dead tree, wanting only a firm shove to topple over.

---

29 Nikolayev, 10.

30 Robert Paul Browder and Aleksandr Fyodorovich Kerensky, *The Russian Provisional Government, 1917: documents, volume 1* (Stanford, CA: Stanford University Press, 1961), 511.

31 Pipes, 439-464.

One: Traditional and Provisional

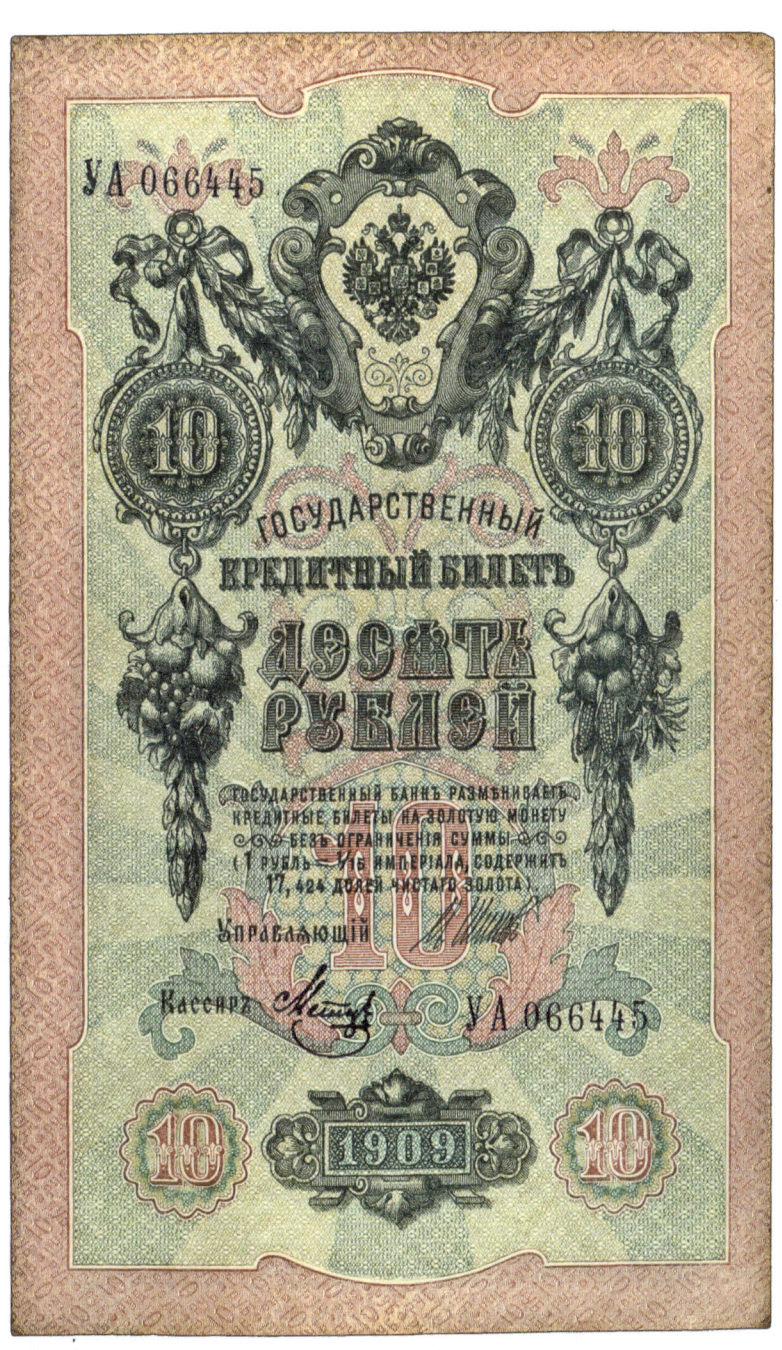

Commie Currency

One: Traditional and Provisional

Commie Currency

One: Traditional and Provisional

Commie Currency

One: Traditional and Provisional

Two: War Communism

During its brief existence, the Provisional government doubled the volume of currency in circulation, and prices tripled.[1] Yet, Lenin pursued economic policies that made Kerensky a benign sage by comparison. In addition, the Communists plunged the country into a ruinous civil conflict.

By their own boasts, the Bolsheviks made war on Russian society and her hapless citizens. The Civil War is covered in some detail in the next two chapters; here we examine the economic warfare of the years 1918–1921. Lenin coined the term "War Communism" to describe this period, in April 1921, just as he changed tactics—to forestall complete economic collapse.

A PLETHORA OF SYMBOLS

Soon after taking control of the capital, Lenin's cohort Leon Trotsky responded to allegations that Germany had financed their revolution. "Why should I need German money? We have printing presses of our own!"[2]

This is typical Trotsky—dissembling, disguised as witticism. In fact, the Kaiser had been supplying funds to the Bolsheviks since 1916. At first, the Germans sent money through go-betweens, such as Alexander Helphand (known by his revolutionary *nom-de-plume,* Parvus). After the Bolsheviks seized power, however, they were paid directly. In January 1918, Lenin, Trotsky, and Cheka chief Dzerzhinsky signed receipts for 12 million rubles.

Later, Lenin had second thoughts about those autographs, rightly fearing the scandal that would ensue if his funding from the Hun should become public knowledge. In consequence, the hapless German clerk who handled the transfer was tortured in Moscow's Butirski prison and then shot, because he was unable to turn over those receipts.[3]

All told, the Kaiser gave the Bolsheviks around 50 million deutsche marks in gold, at that time the equivalent of a million troy ounces, or in modern terms, about 1.4 billion dollars.[4] This sizeable investment greatly assisted the fledgling Communist administration in holding on to power.

Trotsky was correct, however, when he pointed out that the Communists now ran the monetary presses. In 1918, the new régime churned out thirty-three billion rubles, more than doubling the money supply. Over five billion rubles in Romanovski were printed, along with seventeen billion in Dumki and eleven billion in Kerenki, but no currency with Soviet symbols had yet been designed.[5]

Yet, even restricting themselves to the designs of previous regimes, the Bolsheviks still managed to generate a price inflation rate of more than 700%. At the end of 1918, an item that cost one Tsarist ruble in 1913 now commanded 164

---

1   The reader will have noticed that price inflation lagged behind the expansion of the money supply during the tsar's war, but raced ahead under the Provisional. Partly, this was due to the early disappearance of metallic money into hoards. More generally, this is an effect observed in the life cycle of price inflation; once people have come to expect continued price increases, they spend their money as quickly as they can.

2   "One Way To Make Money," *New York Times*, 9 March 1918, 16.

3   Michael Occleshaw, *Dances in Deep Shadows* (New York: Carroll & Graf Publishers, 2006), 3, 40.

4   Pipes, *The Russian Revolution* (New York: vintage Books, 1991), 411.

5   Arthur Arnold, *Banks, Credit, and Money in Soviet Russia* (New York: Columbia University Press, 1937), 80.

Commie Currency

rubles from the continually increasing quantity and variety of money.

Early in 1919, a commission met to choose a design for Soviet currency, but failed to reach consensus (it was still possible to disagree in those days). Plates were discovered bearing a design created, but not implemented, by the Provisionals. These were slapped in the presses and bills printed, beginning in mid 1919.

As shown here in 250-ruble (reverse) and 500-ruble (observe) denominations, the new currency displayed the previous year as their issue date. Moreover, they featured the symbolism of a government that had folded the year before that. Russians took these oddities in stride, and called the bills *Piatakovki,* from the signature, shown on the left of the 250-ruble note, of the "Manager."

The run of the Piatakovki stopped at the 1000-ruble note, but in October 1919 the Bolsheviks broke new ground with a 10,000-ruble "Credit Bill." If you look closely, you will find not one but three swastikas, in the center and under each number.

As before, the symbol was not intended to be racist. Indeed, anti-Semitism was much more prevalent among the Whites, who pointed to highly visible Jewish Bolsheviks (such as Trotsky, whose real name was Bronstein), as evidence of the conspiracy alleged in the notorious tract, *Protocols of the Elders of Zion.* The Communists, however, gave as little thought to the swastika as they did to the eagle, for they were busily occupied in destroying nearly every aspect of the economy.

A TOKEN OF MY ACCOUNTING

Lenin pressed hard for a new form of currency, seeing it as a means of exposing and destroying class enemies. In early 1918 he wrote to I.E. Gukovsky, Commissar of Finance, on his specific requirements. The new money had to carry "a *Soviet* inscription," while retaining "the old text about being exchangeable for gold (the exchange will be suspended by separate decrees)."[6]

But, owing to bureaucratic delays, money with Soviet designs did not appear until March 1919, and first in trifling denominations of one to three rubles as illustrated here. Nor did the lie about gold make it onto the bills; in any case, no one would have believed it.

The new state symbols of hammer and sickle were supposed to represent the twin engines of triumphant socialism—industry and agriculture—that would catch and surpass decadent capitalism. In truth, the hammer represented what was being done to Russia's upper classes, the savers who drove the industrial economy.

In December 1917, holders of safety-deposit boxes had been forced to open them for inspection. Gold, foreign currencies and valuables were confiscated outright, while domestic money and savings were placed in a restricted account that inflation soon rendered worthless. All real estate was nationalized; all government debt was annulled. Lenin called these procedures "looting the looters."

Private and commercial banks were liquidated, almost a moot point since the other measures had already made their mortgages and bonds valueless. The Bolsheviks solved their immediate

---

[6] V.I. Lenin, *Collected Works* (Moscow: Progress Publishers, 1975), 44: 116. It would never have occurred to Lenin that this was blatant fraud.

Two: War Communism

cash-flow problems by sending armed soldiers to banks to seize whatever they could find. Lenin's wife later wrote an account of the procedure:

> We stuffed them ["old sacks" that a bank messenger thoughtfully provided] full to the top with money, swung them on our shoulders and hauled them out to the motor-car. We rode back to the Smolny, beaming.... While waiting for him [Lenin] to come, I sat down on the sacks with a revolver in my hand, 'mounting guard.' I handed the money over to Vladimir Ilyich with great solemnity.... Thus originated our first Soviet budget.[7]

The sickle on these bills represented the armed robbery of the peasant, a process called "requisition." Moscow set quotas for food production, improbably based on what might be possible under the best of conditions. The Red Army took grain, produce, and livestock at gunpoint, leaving colored paper in payment. As Lenin put it, "we actually took from the peasant all his surpluses—and sometimes even a part of his necessaries—to meet the requirements of the army and sustain the workers. Most of it we took on loan, for paper money."[8] This extortion, coupled with bad weather, led to the famine of 1921–1922, in which between one and three million people died.

The bills assert that they are "equal to credit bills." In fact, until the Bolsheviks won the Civil War, communist currency was heavily discounted to Tsarist bills, and circulated at a loss even to Dumki and Kerenki. At times, the premium for Tsarist money was 50 or 60 to 1.

The most significant change that came with the new Bolshevik bills was taxonomic; the new paper is called, just below the seal, "accounting token." Giddy with their success in taking control, the Bolsheviks were entertaining the notion that they could *eliminate money*.

THE TOWER OF BABBLE

In abolishing private property and nationalizing production, the Bolsheviks had destroyed any tax base. By repudiating public debt, they had ensured that no one would be so insane as to loan them money. That left the press.

When Lenin took power in 1917, slightly less than twenty billion rubles circulated; this quantity was tripled by the end of 1918, quadrupled again by the start of 1920, and quintupled yet again by January 1921. (In the following two years, things got really strange, but that story is told in chapter six.)

Making a virtue of necessity, as even radicals are wont to do, the Communists praised inflation as a tool of the revolution. One Soviet economist penned this panegyric:

> "Hail to our printing press.... the machine gun of the Commissariat of Finance that poured fire into the rear of the bourgeois system and that made use of the laws of currency circulation of that regime for the purpose of destroying it and of financing the revolution."[9]

Inflation eroded the power and the will of the propertied class, who were most likely to oppose

---

7 N.K. Krupskaya, *Reminiscences of Lenin* (New York: International Publishers, 1970), 418-419.

8 V.I. Lenin, *Collected Works* (Moscow: Progress Publishers, 1965), 32: 342.

9 E. Preobrazhensky, 1920, in Arnold, 95-96.

Commie Currency

the new order. The writer and future Nobel laureate Ivan Bunin captured the deadening effect of price inflation:

> This is the hellish secret of the Bolsheviks—to kill all sensitivity.... Take the price of bread or beef, for example. 'What? Three rubles a pound!' Then it goes up to a thousand—but there comes an end to the shock and screaming; stupor and passivity take their place. 'What? Seven were hanged?!' 'No, my dear, not seven, but seven hundred!'[10]

Seen in this light, it made perfect sense for the Bolsheviks to use gold to purchase paper and ink from foreign capitalists and print near-worthless currency. During this time, the costs of printing money, an industry that employed 15,000 workers, comprised as much as one-half of the total budget!

Even seven decades later, the Soviets took great pride in having used inflation to wage class warfare, while denying the responsibility for causing it:

> Inflation was induced by the development of barter trade. [The writer is confusing, perhaps deliberately, cause and effect. *After* hyperinflation had become endemic, vendors preferred to trade for other objects of value.] However, in its socio-economic contents emission [printing money] in Soviet Russia differed radically from inflation in the capitalist countries.... Under the conditions of money depreciation capitalist owners of large amounts of paper money were actually deprived of their savings by nationalization of means of production and impossibility to use their money.... [Workers were protected in that] by 1920 93% of wages and salaries were paid in the form of staple commodities [that had been expropriated from peasants].[11]

However, using inflation as a class-war cannon did not solve the fundamental problem Marxists have with money. Although issued by the state, currency can be used in private exchanges. It is simple enough to debase the currency, but the Communists wanted to nationalize exchange, as they had nationalized production.

The rapid abolition of money was made an official goal at the Eighth Party Congress in March 1919. Its place was to be taken by, initially, a system of vouchers and entitlements. The new currency would be, put simply, a token of accounting. It was imagined that, before long, people would have no need of even these, because all things would be free (recall Bukharin). Until then, the necessities of life were to be administered through the workplace.

It followed, as night does day, that people sought employment with whatever department offered the best perks. Salaries had become trivialities; for example, Lenin's monthly wage in 1920 was 6500 rubles, barely enough to "buy thirty cucumbers on the black market."[12]

Lenin was shocked by the resulting rapid growth of Soviet bureaucracies, with their

---

10 Ivan Bunin, *Cursed Days,* trans. Thomas Marullo (London: Phoenix Press, 2000), 103.

11 L.N. Zaitseva, *State Paper Money of RSFSR and USSR* (Moscow: Mezhnumizmatika, 1989), 11.

12 Richard Pipes, *Russia under the Bolshevik Regime* (New York: Vintage Books, 1994), 447. That was at the start of 1920; by the end of the year it had doubled.

Two: War Communism

clumsy acronyms and bizarre names (really, the Commissariat of Enlightenment?). He complained about this unexpected (to him) development, in a letter to G.Y. Sokolnikov:

> All the work of all our economic bodies suffers most of all from bureaucracy. Communists have become bureaucrats. If anything will destroy us, it is this. And for the State Bank it is most dangerous of all to be bureaucratic.[13]

The state expanded, because people needed to eat. Real productivity fell precipitously, while white-collar featherbedding grew by leaps and bounds. It was during this time that the peculiarities that characterized the Soviet Union were set in place. A letter required only nominal postage, but it took ages to arrive. Rent was very cheap, but you could wait years to get into a concrete matchbox slum.

Waiting became endemic as each bureaucrat justified his existence. There is a venerable joke about the man who goes through the process to purchase an automobile, and is told that the car can be picked up in ten years time. He asks if it can be ready in the morning; "you see, the plumber is coming in the afternoon."

Late in 1919, the Bolsheviks introduced the new monetary series, and it was then that the currency acquired its popular name. The Russian word for token is *znak*, so they were called *Sovznaki*. As was now typical, they were marked with the year prior to actual issue. There was, it seems, a queue for everything, even currency.

First issues of the Sovznaki were low-value bills: 15, 30, and 60 rubles. Why use these odd denominations? The most popular Tsarist gold coin was the "Imperial," valued at 15 rubles after the 1897 reform (it was 10 rubles before). Perhaps this value was imitated, consciously or not, to inspire confidence in the new regime's currency. In any event, these denominations were not used again. During the hyperinflation, bills of fifteen and thirty *thousand* appeared, but we are getting ahead of our story there.

Some months into 1920, larger denomination bills were printed. Shown are the 100-ruble and the highest value 10,000-ruble tokens. Tokens of 250, 500, 1000, and 5000 rubles were also issued, but they are similar to these.

The larger bills acquired an additional nickname, from the multilingual slogan printed on them. At this time, the Bolsheviks still dreamed of a worldwide revolution, and to promote this, they printed Marx's motto on their tokens: "Workers of the World, Unite!" It is printed in Russian, English, French, German, Italian, Chinese, and Arabic. Because of that multiplicity of tongues, the tokens were called *Babylonians*.

TWO STEPS FORWARD, ONE STEP BACK

The writings of Karl Marx and Frederich Engels present a theory of history. A process of conflict, called the *dialectic*, is held to further social development via the mechanism of a *thesis* reacting with its *antithesis* and producing a *synthesis*. The final product of this process, the communist society, will not, it is argued, produce an antithesis, because all class contradictions have been resolved. And so, Marxism is a kind of genealogy,

---

13 V.I. Lenin, *Collected Works* (Moscow: Progress Publishers, 1976), 549. Sokolnikov was Commissar of Finance, and was killed in Stalin's purges.

Commie Currency

with its final progeny an immortal creature, one that is supposed to be utopia for the workers.[14]

Marx was happy to pass his life scribbling away in the British Library while sponging off his capitalist friend Engels, but the Bolsheviks took a different approach. These were people whose favorite book was *What is to be Done?* Like Frankenstein, they cobbled together a body and gave it a big jolt, hoping thereby to bring the Soviet utopia to life. Their favorite motto said it all: "Electrification plus the Five-Year Plan equals Communism!"

Lenin and friends liquidated private property, individual and corporate business, the banks and most financial instruments, and placed all these institutions in the hands of state bureaucrats. It followed that the number of functionaries who pushed paper multiplied exponentially, while actual production of goods and services fell precipitously. These were unintended and ironic consequences, for the self-proclaimed men of action.

The results were glaringly disastrous; by 1921, industrial production had fallen to one-fifth of pre-war levels, and Lenin was forced to retreat slightly. In March 1921, the New Economic Policy was proclaimed; forced requisitions were replaced by taxes in kind, and farmers were permitted to sell their remaining wares on the open market. Restrictions limiting the amount of cash an individual could possess were relaxed, and private investment was encouraged. Small-scale capitalists, known as NEP-men, appeared on the streets; shops and cooperatives reopened,

and the economy began to pull back from the precipice.

No attempt was made to reform the flagging currency, however. Even as the Party back-pedaled, a blue-ribbon commission proposed replacing money with coupons based on labor units, to be known as *treds*. Alternately, it was suggested that the values of labor and other production inputs should be quantified in terms of energy, expressed as the *ened*.[15]

Neither of these schemes were enacted, and for the rest of 1921 the government simply continued to turn out Sovznaki. The supply of 1919 tokens leaped from 600 billion to 2 trillion rubles, and this staggering growth was supplemented by the appearance of new issues.

This 50-ruble accounting token was an attempt to placate the small change famine, like the 20-ruble Kerenki it resembles. But the Soviet version had a much smaller purchasing power; when issued in mid-1920 it was worth less than a Provisional kopeck.

In the summer of 1921, new Sovznaki appeared. The smaller denominations, which now included the 1000-ruble token shown here, were printed on only one side. Like other accounting tokens, this one assures the holder that it is "secured by all property of the republic." The currency could not, however, be used to purchase any of the republic's property, now nationalized, and which, of course, had been stolen from its previous owners.

The Babylonians now made their final appearance, because the Bolsheviks had realized that, unlike lemmings, other nations were not about to follow them over the precipice. Postponing the world revolution, they concentrated on building "Socialism in one country." This term

---

14   For a more thorough examination of the prophetic and dogmatic aspects of Marxism and Leninism, see Timothy Buchanan, *Consequences* (Manitou Springs, Colorado: Eagle Mtn. Press, 2010).

15   Arnold, 107, 110.

Two: War Communism

(a contradiction to Marxist theory, which is inherently internationalist) was popularized by Stalin, who was busily laying the groundwork for his eventual domination of that country.

There is an amusing error on the 5000-ruble Babylonian shown here. Marx's slogan is printed in the original German in the top left corner, but the word Proletariat is misspelled. It should read *"Proletarier,"* not *"Proletapier."* It is easy to guess how the mistake happened. The engraver used the Cyrillic letter that gives the sound of the Latin *R* but is written like *P*, and no one noticed, or bothered, to correct it.

The Bolsheviks again upped the ante with higher denomination bills, and increased the volume of circulating notes to over 15 trillion rubles. That figure includes 2 billion in Nikolaevski and Dumki, printed either out of habit or because they still traded at a premium.

This 50,000-ruble note is printed in a soothing shade of green with a display of agricultural cornucopia. In 1921, millions of citizens were facing hunger and even starvation, but the irony of this presentation was probably unintentional.

This starkly simple 100,000-ruble token was the first six-digit bill printed in Russia during the Soviet era. The 50,000 and 100,000 bills were printed only in July and August 1921.[16] As the price index passed through 80,000, the Bolsheviks began to rethink their scheme to abolish money. In late 1921, they made their first, half-hearted, attempts to reform the currency. First, however, we will examine the many and diverse issues of the Russian Civil War.

---

16 Zaitseva, 122.

Two: War Communism

Commie Currency

Two: War Communism

Commie Currency

Two: War Communism

Commie Currency

Two: War Communism

Three: White Guard, Red Blood

There are many historical curiosities in the rise of the Soviet Union, but perhaps none more poignant than this: the Bolsheviks hastened to make peace with Germany, then rushed into a far more ruinous war against their own people.

The Russian Civil War was a complicated affair: nationalists mingled with foreign meddlers; patriots fought alongside opportunists; clear-eyed despots led hapless villagers. Of all the belligerents, only the Bolsheviks possessed a single-minded purpose enforced by a tightly controlled organization. Moreover, they occupied the geographic center, Moscow, from where they could strike in any necessary or expedient direction. These two advantages—the focus of the mind and the hub on the map—proved crucial to their victory.

In those years of civil conflict, currency circulating within the former empire achieved an amazing variety; everyone, it seems, was involved with the literal making of money.

Newly independent nations resurrected ancient symbols. Regional and city administrations worked to mollify the *money hunger* symptomatic of inflation. As territories repeatedly changed hands, rival currencies vanished and then reappeared. White Army commanders had money printed abroad to fund the domestic war. Private institutions resorted to vouchers and tokens to replace scarce small change. Unscrupulous individuals took advantage of the chaos and printed their own money, pocketing the proceeds. All of these currencies, plus the money of the ancient regime, the Provisional government, and the Soviets, circulated at various and volatile discounts to each other. Whew!

And so, the story of civil war money is as complex as the history of the Russian Civil War itself. In this chapter and the next, the tale is told as simply as possible. Rather than adhere to a strict chronology of events, it will be necessary to jump from time to time and place to place. This is fitting, for this is how the war proceeded, fitfully. The main strongholds for the White Guard were located in South Russia and Siberia. But crucial battles occurred in a wide arc: from the Arctic Circle down past the Baltic provinces, through Ukraine to the Black Sea, and across the sea to the land beyond the Caucasus.

EASTERN DRIVE

As there is complexity in the history of the Civil War, so there is controversy to its beginnings. Soviet historians dated the conflict as beginning in the summer of 1918, thereby casting the Whites as assailants on the established, legitimate administration. But the October Revolution was itself an insurrectional attack, albeit farcical; while the *Aurora* fired blank rounds, the Bolsheviks overcame melancholic ministers cowering in their cabinets.

So, the Russian Civil War could be dated from 7 November 1917. One might set the struggle even further back, when the Russian Empire began to disintegrate under the pressures of the Great War. For it was mismanagement of the war that caused the military and the middle class to lose confidence in Nicholas. It was stubborn pursuance of the war that cost Kerensky his position. It was territory lost in the war that hosted the foes of Lenin. It all goes back to the World War, and to Russia's adversary, Germany.

Latvia, Lithuania, Estonia, Poland, Ukraine; these were once and would be future nations, but in 1914 they belonged to the Russian Empire. Germany's misfortune was that she came late to the Age of Empires, when only scraps, mostly in Africa, were left. *Drang nach Osten*, the Drive to the East, was designed to remedy

Commie Currency

that problem—by converting Russian satellites into German protectorates. After the Russian catastrophe at the Battle of Tannenberg[1] in August 1914, the Kaiser's troops advanced into the Polish provinces and up the Baltic coast. By the time of Kerensky's ill-fated offensive in June 1917, the Eastern Front began just west of Riga, ranged southward through western Ukraine, and reached the Black Sea about a hundred miles west of Odessa.

The Germans printed money for the occupied territories; this 3-ruble note was issued on 17 April 1916, in Posen. An important city in medieval Poland, Posen was called Poznań until the Congress of Vienna awarded it to Prussia in 1815. In 1914, Germany intended to construct a tributary state in Poland and a militarized frontier zone in the Baltics.

German authorities envisioned a monetary union of the puppet and the buffers, and used Polish, Latvian, and Lithuanian on the notes (including a warning against counterfeiting, always a problem when currency is cheaply produced). After the Bolsheviks withdrew from the war in early 1918, the German Empire drove farther to the east than they had hoped or planned.

Expecting at any moment the World Revolution, the Communists airily declared a policy of "neither war nor peace," and refused to discuss terms with the Kaiser's representatives. Flabbergasted by this show of insouciance, Germany responded with renewed action on the Eastern Front, hostilities that went unopposed by the dispirited and largely disbanded Russian troops.

Such was the "Comical War," in which a handful of German troops would travel to a town by train, arrive unopposed, plant the flag, and then rush off to the next station. In two weeks, the Kaiser's troops swept through Belarus, Ukraine, the Crimea, and the Donetz basin as far as the Don River. When Trotsky finally agreed (at Lenin's insistence) to the Brest-Litovsk treaty on 3 March 1918, Russia had lost a fourth of her land and people, and three-quarters of her coal mines and iron industry. (As a final gesture of nonchalance, the Russian signatories refused to actually read the treaty.)

These occupied regions served as bases of operation for anti-Bolshevik forces; after the Germans withdrew, locals continued to resist the new regime. One prominent military historian believes that there "need have been no civil war in Russia" if the Bolsheviks hadn't "prevaricated with the Germans over the terms of the peace settlement that would have confirmed their victory."[2]

Even after the November armistice, Germany continued to play a role in Russia's civil conflict. One of the lesser-known wartime incidents is illustrated here with a piece of German-Russian currency printed in Latvia. Germany captured the capital, Riga, in September 1917, and held the city until January 1919. Meanwhile, the Latvian Peasant's Council had declared independence, and sought protection with the British Navy. German troops still occupied southwestern Latvia, and the Allies tolerated this as a bulwark against Red expansion. Led by Graf von der Goltz, the Germans took Mitava in March 1919, and recaptured Riga from the Reds in May, but paused, under political pressure from the Allies.

Intent on establishing a Baltic puppet state, von der Goltz renamed his force the "Western

---

[1] The Russians lost 170,000 men—killed, wounded, or captured—the Germans 12,000.

[2] John Keegan, *An Illustrated History of the First World War* (New York: Alfred Knopf, 2001), 355-6.

Three: White Guard, Red Blood

Volunteer Army," and gave nominal command to a Russian adventurer, Pavel Bermondt, who called himself Prince Avalov. Avalov was a "flamboyant figure" who relieved stress by "emptying his pistol into the ceiling of his quarters."[3] This sort of eccentricity was typical of Civil War adventurers; some other commanders tended to empty their guns into unfortunate bystanders.

Some Latvians fought alongside the prince, some against; the Estonians and Lithuanians attacked Latvia, backed by Anglo-French artillery support; the Reds made trouble wherever they could; it was a confusing mêlée. By December, however, the Western Volunteers were forced out, the other Balts and Bolsheviks withdrew, and Latvians had their own country—at least until 1940.

Incidentally, I visited Latvia shortly after she regained her independence in 1991. Soviet border guards still stood at their posts at the airport, but no longer had any authority. Instead, my entry was recorded in a school notebook, by a young Latvian woman wearing a Yale sweatshirt. Also incidentally, Pavel the Prince, who was born in 1884, lived until 1973. Curiously, his flag is used today in Russia, the white, blue, and red tricolor.

Pavel's 10-mark "Provisional Exchange Token" was printed in Mitava on 10 October 1919, four days after the Volunteers launched their ill-fated attack. It promises, somewhat rashly, that the bearer may exchange the token for real money after 1 April 1920. There must be very few documents that bear both the Russian double eagle and the German iron cross, as does this wistful promise of German money, in the Russian tongue.

THE FAR FROM QUIET DON

In the six months following October, the Bolsheviks attempted to consolidate their power throughout central Russia. In their version (not in the least comic) of a railway war, they relied on the cooperation of local Soviets, assemblies that were entirely socialist but only partly Bolshevik. Peasants understandably responded to Bolshevik slogans: "All Power to the Soviets!" and "Peace, Land, and Freedom!"

Who would have realized that local Soviets would soon fall under strict control from far-off Moscow? Who would have guessed that, in the new order, peace meant ruinous war, land meant nationalization of all property, and freedom meant ruthless suppression of speech and action? The heady dreams of 1917 died when Lenin closed the Constituent Assembly, Russia's final experiment in democracy, on 6 January 1918, an epiphany of Communist repression. In April, Lenin declared, "It can be said with certainty that, in the main, the Civil War is at an end."[4] Lenin was mistaken, for the conflict was just beginning.

Cossack—derived from a Turkish word for migrant—refers to a free-spirited people who settled in the river regions of the Dnieper, which drains into the Black Sea, and the Don, which flows into the Sea of Azov. Even though the Cossacks acknowledged imperial rule, after the fall of the Tsar they attempted to reassert their independence. Ex-Tsarist military officers joined forces with the Don's elected chief, Ataman Kaledin, to form the Volunteer Army. Their first effort was disastrous; the Cossacks lost their

---

3 W. Bruce Lincoln, *Red Victory* (New York: Simon and Schuster, 1989), 294.

4 Lenin, *Collected Works* (Moscow: Progress Publishers, 1972), 27: 229.

Commie Currency

capital, Novocherkassk, to the Reds in February 1918, and their ataman shot himself in despair.

The remnants of the Volunteers marched south, regrouped, elected an experienced general as ataman, and began to win battles. Ironically, the Whites, most of whom were ex-Tsarist Army, were assisted by German troops, who blocked Red railways and supplied arms. Alternate routes from Moscow went through Tsaritsin, on the Volga River, but when that city was besieged, the Reds were unable to relieve their forces. The Kuban, on the east shore of the Black Sea and north of the Caucasus Mountains, became an anti-Bolshevik stronghold, headquarters of the South Army.

This 250-ruble note was issued in Rostov-on-the-Don, gateway to the Kuban. The city was controlled by Bolshevik sailors in December 1917, and the battle to capture Rostov was the first joint effort of the Cossacks and White officers. The fight began on 9 December, a feast-day of St. George, and is considered the first major battle of the Civil War.

The Volunteer Army managed to take the city, but Rostov fell again to the Reds on 23 February 1918. The Cossacks' southward retreat from Rostov, the "Ice March," became an epic tale of suffering and hardening. The reinvigorated Whites recaptured Rostov in May, with German help, and it remained in their hands until the evacuation to Crimea in 1920 (next chapter).

The portrait on this bill is that of Matvei Platov. Born in 1751 in a Cossack village, he rose through military ranks to become one of the Tsar's leading generals. His cavalry was instrumental in the defeat of Napoleon in 1812, and General Platov was celebrated throughout Europe.

Platov is flanked by the Roman and Greek goddesses of war, Minerva and Athena. The Whites often used classical references on their currency, as an assertion of heritage and legitimacy. Athena is said to have appeared from Zeus' brow, fully ready for battle with sword and shield as shown here. Minerva clutches a symbol of Roman power, the axe bound with sticks. She is gazing upward at the double-headed eagle, minus, you will notice, the Romanov crown. White ambivalence regarding the monarchy weakened their cohesiveness, and was an important factor in their ultimate defeat.

BALTIC SIDESHOW

Besides fending off German attempts to establish a puppet state, the Estonians provided support for the Northwest Army. This group was originally called the Northern Army, but that title proved too grandiose for an outfit that never numbered more than 16,000 men. Still, the Northwest Army provided the Bolsheviks with moments of gut-clenching fear, and stood, briefly, at the center of the war.

It began in Pskov, an ancient Russian city about 200 miles south of Petrograd. The Bolsheviks had taken control of Pskov just one week after their coup, but the city was occupied by Germany under the Brest-Litovsk Treaty.

In October 1918, General Aleksey Vandam formed the Northern Russian Volunteer Army. Born to a humble family named Edrikhin, Vandam worked his way up the ranks, serving in military intelligence and writing papers on strategic analysis. For his perspicacity in foreseeing future antagonisms between Russia, China, and

Three: White Guard, Red Blood

the "Anglo-Saxons," he has recently been characterized as the founder of Russian geopolitics."[5]

Vandam issued this 50-ruble "Pskov District Treasury Credit Note" (signature lower left). Within six weeks, however, he lost command of his army. The Regional Government was proclaimed on 2 November, but the Germans withdrew after the armistice of the 11th day of the 11th month, and the Reds re-entered the city on the 25th. Having lost German support, the Whites then fled.

The Northwest Army re-grouped in Estonia, under the command of Alexander Rodzyanko. Hailing from a well-known family, with an uncle in the Duma, General Rodzyanko served in the tsarist cavalry. He assumed command in February 1919, and retook Pskov in May. Vandamm notes still circulated, but Rodzyanko's staff convinced him that more money was needed.

The general spoke to a partisan leader named Bulak-Bulakovich, who was busy printing fake Kerenki. (The 20-ruble and 40-ruble Kerenki from chapter one were found in Estonia during demolition of an old building; one or more may be his.) These two apparently argued; in his memoirs Rodzyanko complained that Bulak-Bulakovich was a "counterfeiter and a scoundrel."

Rodzyanko then decided to print his own money, in denominations of 1 to 10 rubles, produced in Revel (now Tallinn, Estonia). This 3-ruble note features St. George slaying the dragon, an image that was so popular the Reds even used it, on a poster featuring Trotsky as the saint!

The bills were, of course, called *Rodzyanki*, and are quite attractive, being drawn in the Empire style. But the money was a failure nonetheless. It was accepted only in the territory controlled by the Northern Army, and even then at a steep discount.[6] Apparently, people preferred fake Kerenki over genuine Rodzyanki.

In June 1919, the Northern Army became the Northwest Army, with General Nicholas Yudenich commanding. He needed money for a planned offensive against Petrograd. Admiral Kolchak, commander of the Whites in Siberia (next chapter), thought such an attack might draw Soviet troops away from his front, and advanced Yudenich 860,000 British pounds.

Secured by Sterling, bills were printed in Sweden, with a 25-ruble example shown here. Yudenich pegged the value of his currency at 40 rubles to one pound, an exchange rate eight times more favorable to the ruble than what was then prevailing. He also promised that, three months after he occupied Petrograd, the bearer could exchange the bills for Russian banknotes.

Naturally, the bills were popularly known as *Petrogradki*. Note the appearance of the axe bound with rods, behind the text promising the note's value. Used also on the Rostov note, this Roman symbol is, in Latin, the *fasces*, the etymon of the twentieth-century word *fascism*.

The general was overly optimistic and the Northwestern Army never captured Petrograd, though it was not for lack of trying. Petrograd had ceased to serve as the capital of Russia when Lenin fled from the German advance (they were 100 miles away), some 17 months earlier. But the city still had great importance, and the Reds panicked when the Whites advanced to within

---

5 Sergey Ponamarev, "General Vandam, the Forgotten Founder of Russian Geopolitics," *Security Index* 1 (81), vol. 13:147.

6 Adapted from R.V. Nikolayev, *Money, Time, Power* (St. Petersburg: Petersburg Collector, 2002), 12-16.

Commie Currency

sight of St. Isaac's Cathedral. Lenin's suggestion (from a distance) was to mobilize the workers, encouraging them by deploying machine guns at their backs.[7]

Trotsky arrived with more troops, the Whites having failed to cut the railway, and claimed credit for the ensuing victory against the "guard-dogs of the counter-revolution." In the end, the Bolsheviks found it necessary to deploy 250,000 men to defeat 14,440.

In spite of that, the battle was a near thing, and might have turned out differently if the Allies had provided assistance. British tanks were present, but were withheld from the final assault, and the British Navy was held back, in Latvia. This is one example of Western ambivalence in the Russian War, with more to follow.

The defeated White Guard withdrew to Estonia, where they were first placed in refuge camps, then disbanded. General Yudenich retired to Paris where, like other ex-pats, he wrote his memoirs. Unlike most other refugees, he could afford Paris.

In April 1920, the general was arrested in Finland and accused of trying to take large sums of Petrogradki abroad. His successful defense was that he was simply selling what was by then worthless currency to collectors for small sums (5 marks would buy 1000 rubles), and, as you see, the money did wind up in collections. But an expatriate newspaper in Prague later reported that Nicholas Yudenich opened an account in a French bank, and deposited nine million francs.[8] It seems the General had taken advantage of the exchange rate he had established, while he still could.

I AM THE WALRUS

The conflict in Russia's far north was, Petrograd aside, a sideshow, of trifling importance militarily. Its significance is that of demonstrating Western attitudes; the Allies—Britain, France, and the United States—appeared ambivalent in motives and ambiguous in actions.

Until late 1918, their main interest lay in supporting any Russian administration that might continue to draw German attention to the Eastern Front. It is not generally appreciated now that, in the spring of 1918, the Central Powers seemed to be winning. The Allies were desperate to give the Germans cause to shift some of their forces back to the East. This motivation vanished with the November armistice.

Regarding Communism *per se*, the Bolsheviks found many fellow travelers in the West, those people to whom Lenin referred, famously, as "useful idiots." Typical of these was a British MP named Wedgwood, who spoke of his "wonderfully enthusiastic" meetings with workers, and derided British intervention as "class war." He further proclaimed, "If this is going to be a class war, that [Communism] is my side."

Opposing Wedgwood in parliamentary debate was Winston Churchill, who warned, "We are bound to take sides…. Neither can we remain indifferent to the general aspect of Bolshevism. Bolshevism is not a policy; it is a disease. It is not a creed; it is a pestilence."[9] Feelings and temper often ran high over the "Russian question"; perhaps for this reason, policy and action proceeded helter-skelter.

The origin of Allied intervention in northern Russia is itself confusing; technically, it began

---

7   This technique was widely used in WWII, with NKVD troops as "blocking brigades."

8   Nikolayev, 91–97.

9   Michael Kettle, *The Road to Intervention* (New York: Harper & Collins, 1981), 2:394, 396–97.

Three: White Guard, Red Blood

with a Bolshevik invitation. During the German "Comical War," Trotsky fretted about military stockpiles at Murmansk, 150 miles inside the Arctic Circle, and agreed to Allied protection. The Brits landed marines in Murmansk and, in August 1918, a flotilla arrived in Archangelsk.

Fifty American marines landed with the flotilla; 100 times that many arrived a month later. These northern ports were to be used to disembark the Czech Corps (see below); Trotsky approved of this plan. Some Allied leaders also entertained the wistful hope that reactivation of the Eastern Front, using Czechs against Germans, might somehow lead to the fall of the Bolshevik government.

But North Russia was never considered seriously as a base from which to topple the Communists, being too far from Moscow via very poor railways. After the Czechs developed other ideas, and the Great War ended, the Allies could find no justification for their presence, and departed in the autumn of 1919.

The far North suffered badly from money hunger. The various currencies being cranked out so frantically in the capital tended not to travel well, so in February 1918, the local State Bank began to issue "checks." The highest denomination printed was 25 rubles, as illustrated here. It is a lovely piece of art, in soothing tones of green and featuring two of the Arctic's best-loved creatures, the polar bear and the walrus. These checks were accepted throughout the region, if not enthusiastically; they were called *Morzhovki*, Russian for walruses.[10]

When the Allies arrived, they didn't want to interfere with local finances, but there was a problem. Most of the Morzhovki had been spent to the south, and nearly 80% of the currency was in Red hands. So the authorities required locals to "register" their money with the bank and have it stamped. There is a Romanov double eagle stamped in red ink on the reverse of this bill, with the name of the re-issuing bank and its cashier.[11] The stamp defaces an otherwise nice depiction of an angel or military saint trampling the devil.

After the arrival of foreign troops, the money shortage worsened, forcing an extensive series of new bills in late 1918. These were issued by the Northern Provisional Government, headed by N.V. Chaikovsky.

Here is a politician who consistently backed the losing cause, yet always landed on his feet. As President of the Free Economic Society, he exhorted Russians to spend their savings on the ill fated "liberty loan" (chapter 5). He was a leader in the Popular Socialists, but left town before they were smashed by the Bolsheviks. He then joined a socialist administration in Archangelsk. After a mysterious coup, apparently encouraged by the occupying Allies, Chaikovsky was the only socialist left in office. Finally, long before the Reds retook Archangelsk, Chaikovsky departed for the much more congenial climate of Paris, in order to participate in the 1919 Peace Conference.

Chaikovsky's money was printed in London, and made to follow Tsarist models as much as possible, in an effort to inspire confidence. Notice how closely this example resembles the one-ruble note in the first chapter. One difference is the bold title at the head of the bill, reading "Northern Russia." Another is the guarantee of exchange printed below the denomination. Forty rubles are valued at one-pound sterling,

---

10   "Walrus" is also the slang term for those people who like to swim in January.

11   Nikolayev, 78-81.

Commie Currency

the same rate that Yudenich arranged, and far above the market rate for rubles.

The inhabitants of the region had little love for the Bolsheviks, and it took the Reds almost six months to pacify the area after the departure of the Allies. In the meantime, speculators bought up *Angliski* at cheap rates from illiterate peasants, sending the currency abroad in exchange for pounds.[12] I do not know if Chaikovsky gained from this, but considering his record, I would not be surprised.

THE HOUSE OF SPECIAL PURPOSE

In histories of the Russian Civil War, the Czech Corps is often presented as a sort of "wild card," implying unpredictable volatility. True, the twists of history are often unpredictable; think of the events in Eastern Europe in 1989, or the U.S. election of 2000. In this case, however, the Czechs acted in accordance with their interests; it was the other participants who were confused, projecting their wishes onto the Czechs.

In 1914, Bohemia was a part of the Austria-Hungarian Empire; Czechoslovaks were drafted and sent to the Eastern Front. Some of these soldiers preferred not to fight fellow Slavs; they crossed the lines and were organized as the Russian Czech Corps. Their ranks increased with Czech POWs, bringing their numbers to 40,000 well-disciplined and motivated fighters.

After the Revolution, the question arose: what to do with them? Lenin had promised an end to the war, but they couldn't be sent home; the Germans were in the way. France, reeling under the spring offensive, proposed sending them to the Pacific port of Vladivostok and thence, somehow, to join the Allies on the Western Front. England agreed, in principle, but wanted to ship some of the Corps via Archangelsk. Paris and London both thought that the Americans, just then joining the war, should provide the ships. Lenin simply wanted to be rid of them; there wasn't much sympathy for Bolshevism among the Czechs.

Unit by unit, the Corps began to move east. Decrepit trains, packed with well-armed men who knew only that they were headed away from their homes, traveled by fits and starts on the Trans-Siberian Railway. On 14 May 1918, one of these trains stopped in Chelyabinsk, in the Ural Mountains. From an adjacent train or building, a disgruntled Hungarian prisoner threw a heavy metal object, striking a Czech soldier in the head and killing him. The Czechs retaliated by hanging the Hungarian, and then took over the town. Reacting hysterically, Trotsky issued orders to shoot the Czechs "on sight."

That tore it; the Corps threw their lot in with the Whites, and soon controlled the rail line. The Trans-Siberian was the only route from Moscow to Siberia, so the Corps gave new life to the faltering anti-Bolshevik movement in the Far East. Moreover, their presence led to increased Allied intervention: British, American, and even Japanese.

The conflict in Siberia is discussed in the next chapter, but another consequence of the braining in Chelyabinsk took place much closer to that town. About 120 miles away lay Yekaterinburg, which at the time was hosting a famous prisoner. Nicholas Romanov and his family, along with their doctor and several servants, were confined in a house belonging to an engineer named Ipatiev.

In July, the Romanovs could hear firing as the Whites moved closer; early on the 17th they were herded into the basement and murdered.

---

12   Nikolayev, 85-90.

Three: White Guard, Red Blood

Nicholas himself died instantly; apparently every member of the firing squad wanted to dispatch him. The girls—Olga, Tatiana, Marie, and Anastasia—were the last to die; bullets bounced off the diamonds sewn into their clothing as they ran screaming around the room.

In their notice announcing the execution of the ex-Tsar, local authorities blamed the Czech Corps for forcing them to act, but pretended that the family had been safely moved. Moscow in turn blamed the Yekaterinburg Soviet for acting without orders, but Trotsky's diary proves otherwise. In it, Trotsky wrote that Sverdlov, head of the Central Executive Committee, mentioned "in passing" that Lenin and he had decided to have the whole family killed.[13] For Sverdlov's part, Yekaterinburg was soon renamed in his honor. The Ipatiev house was known as "the house of special purpose," and stood in Sverdlovsk until 1976, when the local party boss, Boris Yeltsin, had it bulldozed.

This is a 2-kopeck voucher issued by the University of the Urals, around the time of its founding in 1920 in Yekaterinburg, for use in the cafeteria, by students or staff. It was valid only with the applied purple stamp of the "Executive Bureau of the University Profession." True, two kopecks was a trifle in those inflationary times, but prices were held artificially low in employment commissaries, where meals could be purchased only with coupons such as this one. Presumably, two kopecks paid for lunch; I leave the quality of the food to your imagination.

---

13   Richard Pipes, *The Russian Revolution* (New York: Vintage Books, 1991), 770.

BEYOND THE CAUCASUS

South of the expansive Russian steppes, and north of the Anatolian plateau, there is a land seemingly wedged into place, between the Black and the Caspian Seas. Across the top of this Eurasian bridge, march the highest mountains of the continent, spanning 930 miles between the waters and topping out at 18,000 feet. On the other side of this natural barrier are the territories known as Transcaucasia, literally, beyond the Caucasus: Armenia, Azerbaijan, and Georgia. Georgia touches the Black Sea, Azerbaijan the Caspian, while Armenia is tragically adjacent to Turkey.

Pursuant to the Brest-Litovsk Treaty, these ancient lands formed the Transcaucasian Federation but, within weeks, each declared full independence. These nations endured only so long as circumstances kept the Bolsheviks at bay, on the other side of the Caucasus.

Azerbaijan marks the easternmost point of Europe, an obscure bit of trivia but the pride of the Azeris. The name for this land is derived from the Persian word for fire, *Azer*, and refers to the blazes that often flare up from the many natural oil seeps. The Zoroastrians worshipped fire, and Azerbaijan was a hotbed, so to say, of that religion, but with the arrival of the Tatars, the Azeris adopted Islam.

In the 19th and early 20th centuries, the world's largest developed reserves of oil lay below the sticky sands of Azerbaijan. Alfred Nobel may be best known for the eponymous prizes, but his family earned the bulk of their fortune from Azeri oil. The presence of so many oil field workers provided support for Bolshevism in the earliest stage of the civil war, and the Reds briefly controlled Baku.

Commie Currency

In July 1918, however, the "26 Commissars" were led away to be shot (becoming Red martyrs in the process), and were replaced by the nationalist Musavat administration, propped up by Turkey. But this fledgling nation was doomed by her suspicion of the Whites, who refused to guarantee independence for Azerbaijan, and by her border war against neighboring Armenia. As soon as the Reds could advance troops beyond the mountains, they easily toppled the Musavat government, in April 1920.

This is a 50-ruble note issued by the Baku Soviet during their brief reign. These were only printed during the second fortnight of July 1918, but the commissars managed to pump out 38 million rubles in that time, in denominations of 10, 25, and 50 rubles. It is an attractive currency, displaying the Tsarist-era city seal of three flames. Below is a view of Baku Bay, with its ships and oil derricks, along with symbols of industry and local fruits.

The bill is signed by People's Commissar Nariman Narimanov, who managed to avoid the fate of his fellow commissars. He did lead a nice funeral for them when the Bolsheviks returned in 1920, complete with the Revolutionary March. Narimanov later ascended to the Executive Committee in Moscow; fortunately for him, he died of natural causes in 1925, before Stalin's purges.

Lenin and Trotsky blamed a British agent named Teague-Jones, wrongly, for the martyred commissars, and issued a *fatwa* against him. That poor man spent the rest of a long life in hiding from Soviet agents.

Armenia's history is more tragic than her neighbor. It was one of the earliest nations to become Christian, perhaps the very first. However, the Armenian Church split from mainstream Orthodoxy after the Council of Chalcedon, and the country fell to Arab invaders in the 7th century. In the 19th century, Eastern Armenia willingly joined the Russian Empire, but the rest of Armenia was held by the Ottomans.

In the last decade of that century, Sultan Abdul Hamid presided over the deaths of some 200,000 Armenians. After taking power in 1908, the Young Turks also carried out bloody purges. The World War gave them cover, and by 1916, perhaps two million innocent people had been systematically murdered. It was the world's first holocaust; a quarter-century later, when dealing with squeamish objections over the murder of Jews, Hitler would respond, "Who today remembers the Armenians?"

Surrounded by her enemies, tiny Armenia was unable to hold on to the independence declared in May 1918. Promises were made at the Paris peace conference of 1919, and then broken. The Bolsheviks colluded with Turkey as they would later with Hitler, even declaring Ataturk to be their "socialist brother." The Reds and the Turks partitioned Armenia, setting borders that remain today. Though temporarily delayed by events in Ukraine, the Soviet government in Armenia was in place by the end of 1920.

When the short-lived Transcaucasian Federation split up, Armenia found herself forced, willy-nilly, to produce her own currency. "Armenian checks" were duly prepared, but both quality and quantity were lacking, so, in late 1919, money was ordered from the London firm of Waterlow and Sons.

This became another case where currency was produced for one régime, but used by another. After taking control, the Soviets decided to issue the bills, but did so at a premium of 100 to 1 over locally produced money. The Reds printed money in mid-1921, which was supposed to circulate at parity with the *Londonski*, as the bills were

Three: White Guard, Red Blood

naturally known. But the foreign bills enjoyed a premium of 1000 to 1500 percent over the Soviet output, and it took months for the Bolsheviks to retire the Londonski.

One of Waterlow's creations (their name is in fine print at the foot) is illustrated here. This attractive 100-ruble note is denominated in Armenian, Russian, and French. The stylized eagles at top recall the Arshakid dynasty, which ruled Armenia from AD 62 to 428, during which time the country became Christian. The mountain is Ararat, traditionally known as the resting place for Noah's Ark, and a compelling symbol for Armenia's Christians. When the Bolsheviks seized power, they ceded Mount Ararat to Turkey, who, to the everlasting dismay of Armenians, retains the holy site today.

THE GEORGIAN AND THE GEORGIAN QUESTION

Georgia enters historical awareness with the myth of Jason and the Argonauts. The Golden Fleece may have had its literal basis in a device used in Colchis (western Georgia) to extract gold from the rivers. Flumes were lined with fleece to catch flakes. Georgia became Christianized early, and entered into the Byzantine sphere.

The region fiercely resisted Muslim aggression, enjoying periods of autonomy unhappily interspersed with times of occupation, by the Seljuks and, later, the Tatars. Georgia allied herself with Russia in the 18th century, and was soon after annexed.

Georgia was occupied by German forces from Brest-Litovsk until the Armistice, and afterwards governed by the Mensheviks. With that administration, Georgia earned the tepid endorsement of Britain and the other Allies.

Like other countries in the region, Georgia won recognition from the Allied Council in Paris, but this only made Moscow more circumspect in laying plans for re-conquest. Economic conditions in Russia in 1921 necessitated foreign aid, and Lenin hesitated to offend the Allies by invading Georgia. But Stalin pressed hard for intervention in his native land, and in February, claiming to respond to an appeal by a phony rebel group, the Reds took Tbilisi, the capital. The Mensheviks continued to resist, but Turkey threatened to attack and Georgia capitulated to Moscow, on 18 March 1921.

This is a 500-ruble note of the ill-fated Republic of Georgia, featuring their much-loved Queen Tamara. A strong leader, she led the country in victories against the Turks. A pious believer, she summoned a council to solve disagreements within the Georgian Church, and supported monasteries on Mount Athos. Her rule, from 1184 to 1212, is often called "The Golden Age of Georgia." Her portrait on this bill is laced with Byzantine iconography, including the throne, bolster pillows, and the columned arch. St. George appears above Saint Tamara.

Of the three Transcaucasian nations, Georgia had retained her independence the longest. But in 1921, Stalin and fellow Georgian Ordzhonikidze re-integrated the three, and ran them as a personal kingdom. In 1922, the framework for what would become the Union of Soviet Socialist Republics was devised, and Stalin proposed that the Transcaucasian countries be kept together in the new union.

Other Georgian Communists strongly objected, feeling themselves the equal of Ukraine or Belarus. It was just at this time that Lenin's suspicions of Stalin boiled over. Lenin decided to confront Stalin with the "Georgian Question" at the upcoming Twelfth Party Congress, hoping

Commie Currency

with this issue to discredit Stalin and remove him from power. Lenin even told Trotsky that he was "preparing a bomb" to toss against the Georgian.

Desperately playing for time, Stalin postponed the start of the Party Congress, and his gamble paid off. On 10 March 1923, Lenin had his third stroke. Though he lived another ten months, he was little more than a vacant-eyed idiot in a wheelchair, a drooling object of pilgrimage for his fellow Bolsheviks. Freed from the one adversary who could defeat him, Joseph Stalin resumed what was now an inexorable climb to complete dictatorship as the undisputed "Great Leader."

This is a "monetary token" issued by the Transcaucasian Soviet Federation of Socialist Republics, Stalin's portmanteau, which printed currency only in 1923 and 1924. Ironically, the house of the Georgian Parliament is portrayed; until 1991, that body was merely Moscow's pawn.

The bill's denomination is an astounding, but nonetheless miniscule, 100 million rubles, with titles in Georgian, Armenian, Azeri, and Russian. The history of the hyperinflation that plagued both sides of the Caucasus is explored in chapter six. But first, we must backtrack a bit to examine the Civil War in Ukraine, Siberia, and the Crimea.

Three: White Guard, Red Blood

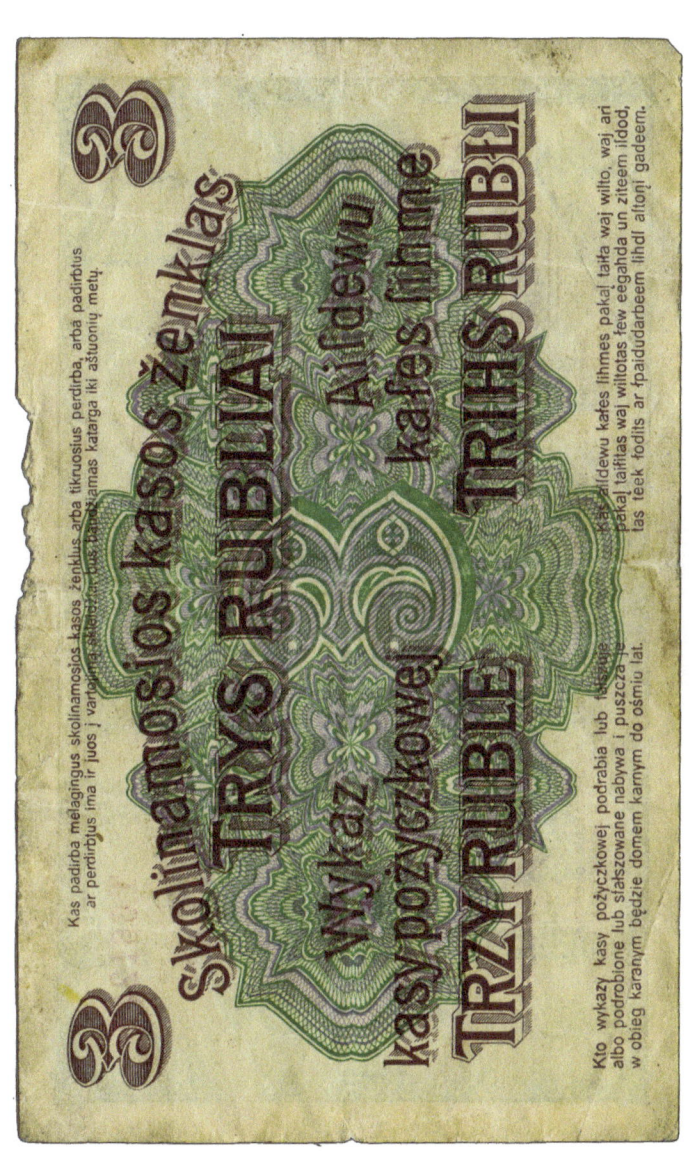

Commie Currency

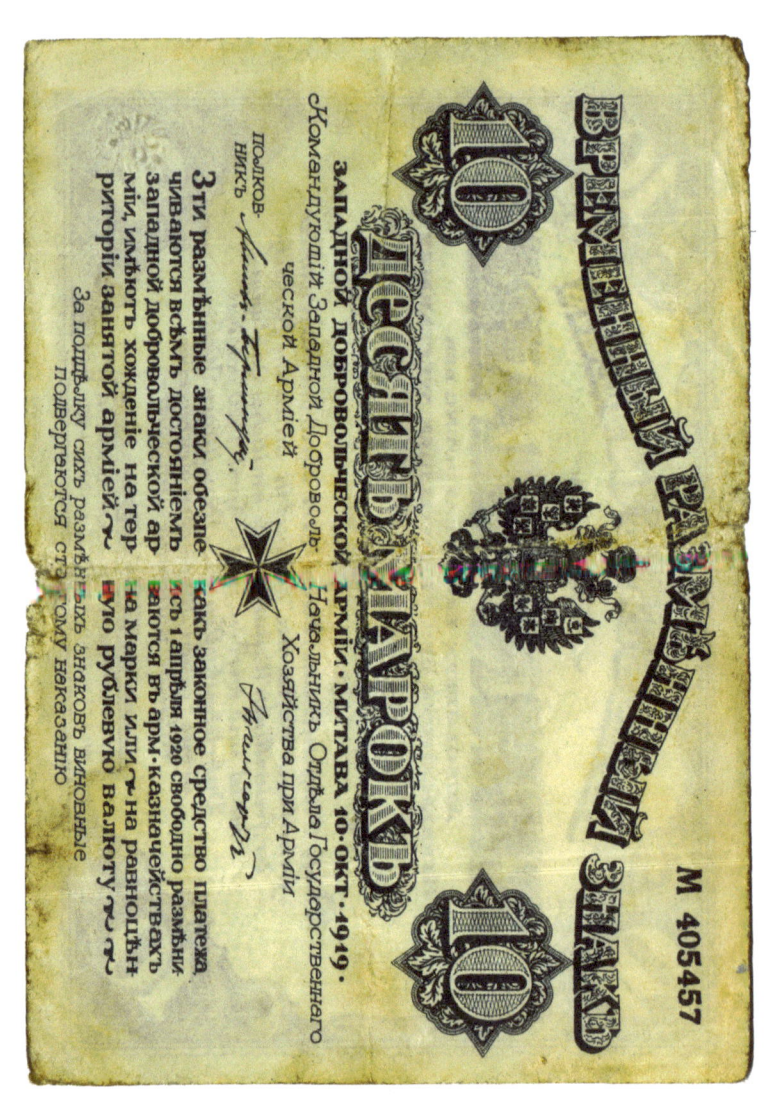

Three: White Guard, Red Blood

Commie Currency

Three: White Guard, Red Blood

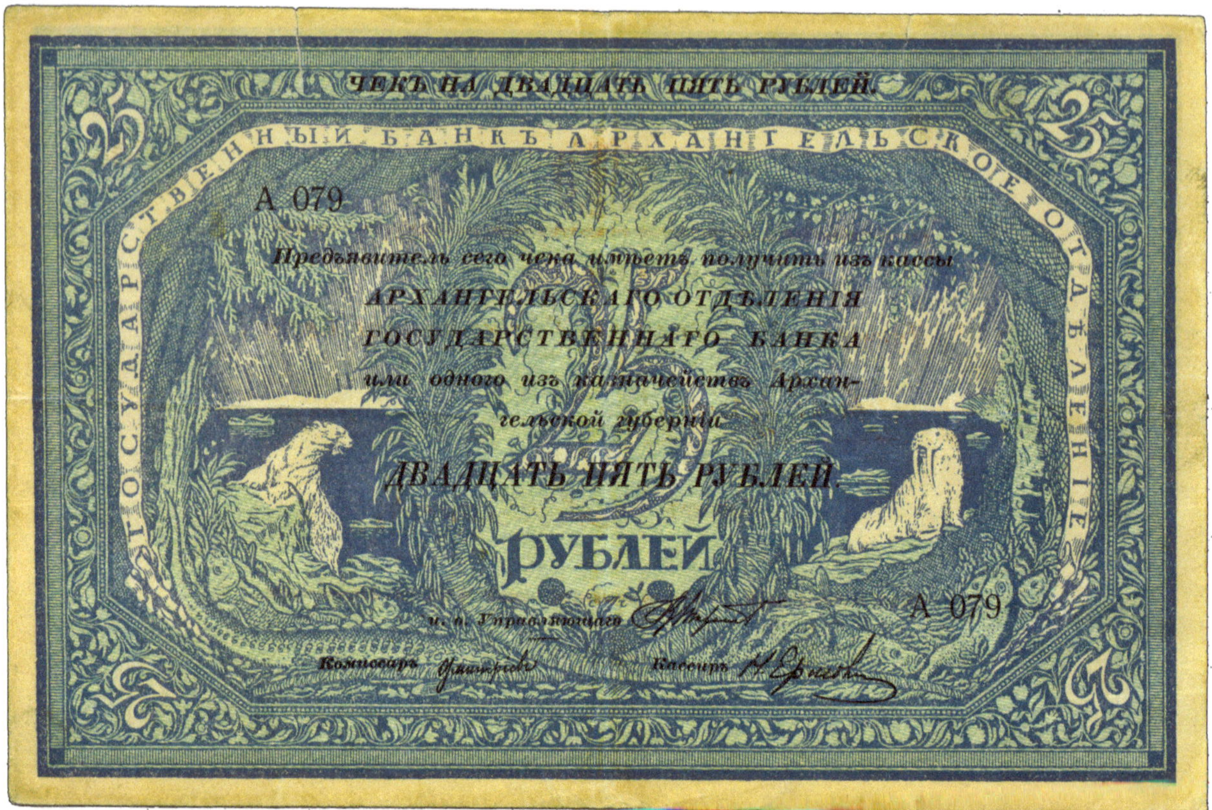
ЧЕКЪ НА ДВАДЦАТЬ ПЯТЬ РУБЛЕЙ.
ГОСУДАРСТВЕННЫЙ БАНКЪ АРХАНГЕЛЬСКОЕ ОТДѢЛЕНІЕ
А 079
Предъявитель сего чека имѣетъ получить изъ кассы
АРХАНГЕЛЬСКАГО ОТДѢЛЕНІЯ
ГОСУДАРСТВЕННАГО БАНКА
или одного изъ казначействъ Архангельской губерніи
ДВАДЦАТЬ ПЯТЬ РУБЛЕЙ.
РУБЛЕЙ
А 079
Комиссаръ
Кассиръ

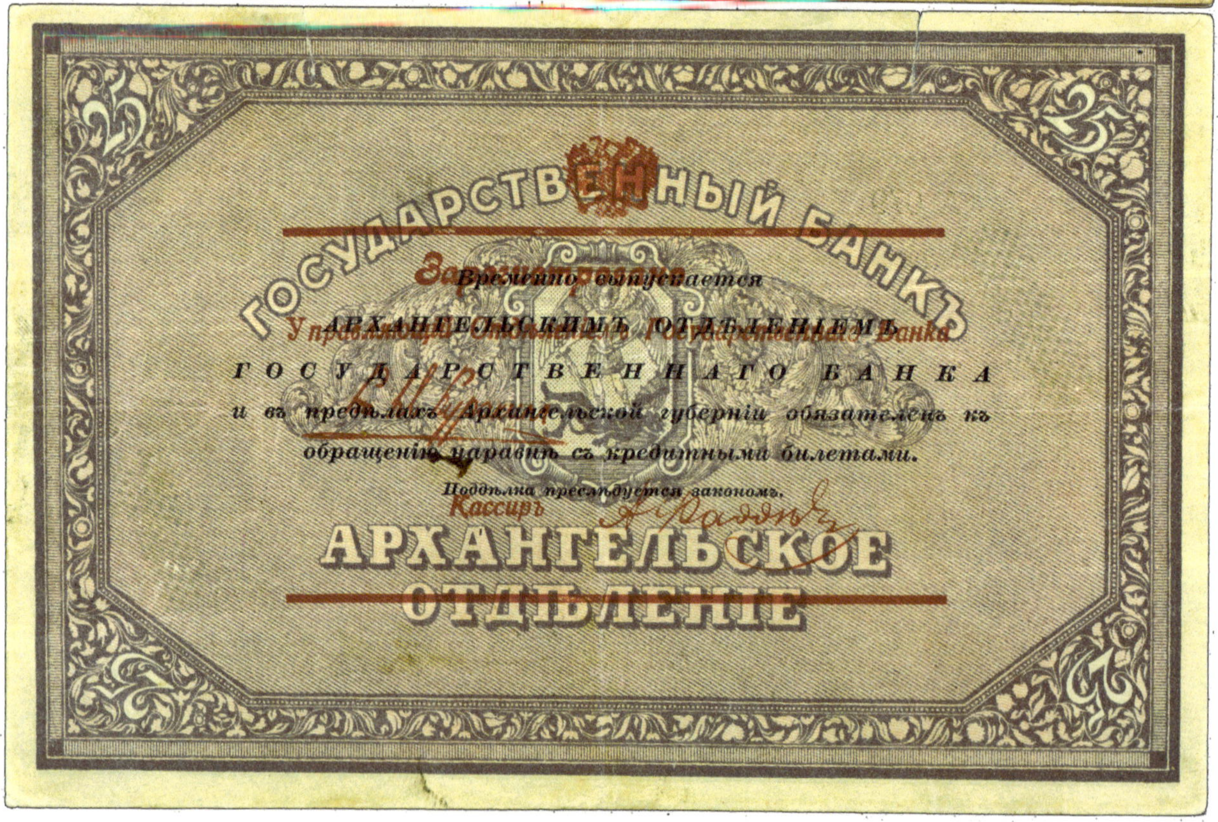
ГОСУДАРСТВЕННЫЙ БАНКЪ
Временно выпускается
АРХАНГЕЛЬСКИМЪ ОТДѢЛЕНІЕМЪ
ГОСУДАРСТВЕННАГО БАНКА
и въ предѣлахъ Архангельской губерніи обязателенъ къ обращенію наравнѣ съ кредитными билетами.
Кассиръ
АРХАНГЕЛЬСКОЕ ОТДѢЛЕНІЕ

Three: White Guard, Red Blood

Commie Currency

Three: White Guard, Red Blood

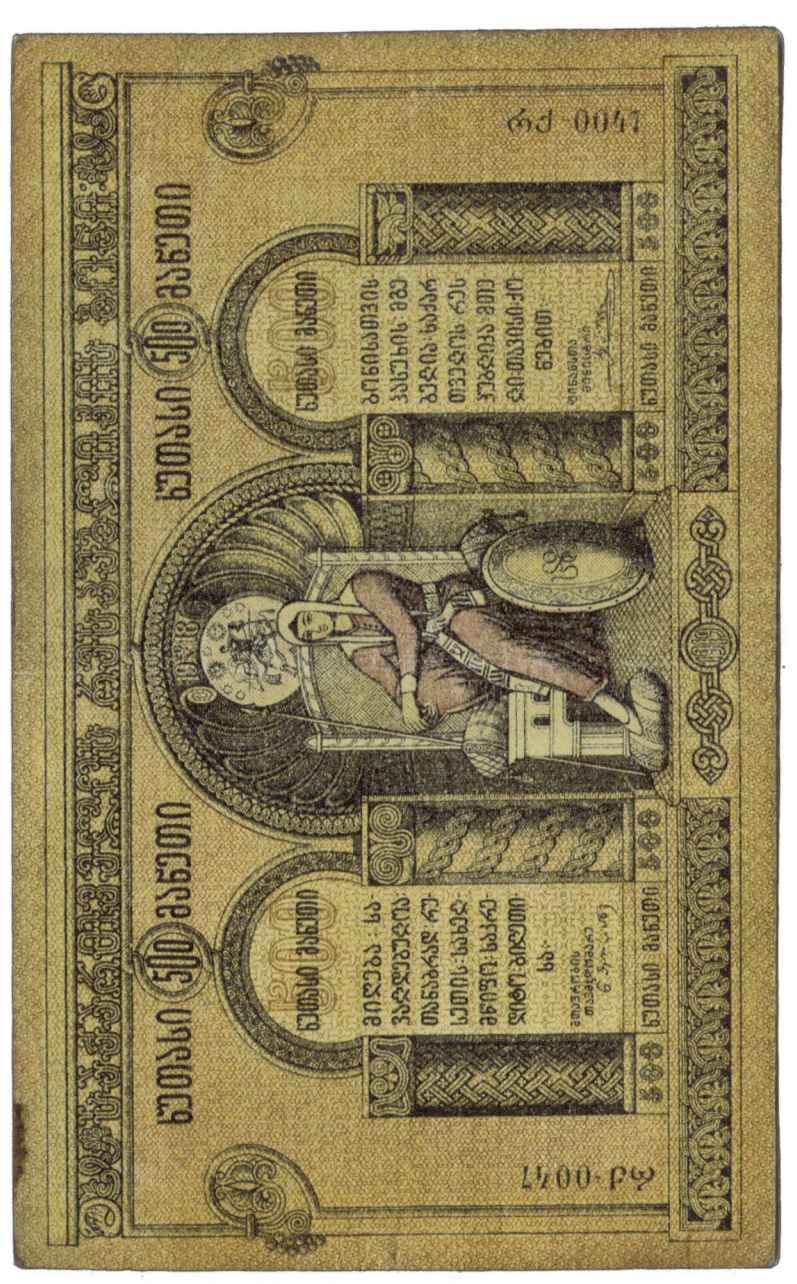

Commie Currency

Four: Main Enemy

During the half-century Cold War, the Soviet Union referred to the United States as *Glavni Vrak*, the "Main Enemy." Use of the phrase was especially popular in the 1980s, as counterpoint to President Reagan's label of the USSR as the "evil empire." The previous chapter focused on areas and personalities of the Russian Civil War that, while interesting, were generally peripheral to the conflict. Now, it is time to look at the main enemies of nascent Bolshevism, and at the primary theaters of action: Ukraine, Siberia, the second battle for the Don, and the final act in the Crimea.

TALE OF TWO CITIES

The Black Sea port of Odessa was founded by Empress Catherine II, who admired the Greek hero Odysseus but wanted a feminine version of the name. However, it has never been an effeminate town, but rather a raw and booming frontier. Mark Twain, writing *Innocents Abroad*, remarked that he felt right at home there.

In 1905, Odessa hosted an insurrection that grew into one of the golden legends of Soviet mythology. Sailors aboard the imperial battleship *Potemkin* mutinied when they were fed maggot-ridden rations, and sought support from the citizens of Odessa. Demonstrators assembled on the Potemkin Steps[1] and were fired upon by Tsarist troops. This incident later became the subject of a seminal film by Sergei Eisenstein, which has been both emulated and satirized. Incidentally, the revolt fizzled and the sailors sought refuge in Romania.

In 1917, Odessa declared herself a Soviet Republic, but that polity was easily brushed aside by German troops during the Comical War. The city was placed, nominally, under the administration of one of the transient governments of Ukraine, but in fact the occupiers retained control.

With the Armistice, the Germans left, and on 18 December, France moved into the vacuum. But within three months, word came of an advancing partisan force, backed by the Bolsheviks and led by an anarchist named Grigorev. As this group neared Odessa, the French decided to cut and run, leaving a distraught and unprotected populace. The locals had reason to be concerned, especially the large contingent of Jews; Grigorev was well known as a looter and anti-Semitic sadist. The April retreat, along with a similar debacle in Sevastopol, comprised France's only direct involvement in Allied intervention.

If France was trivial to the conflict, Odessa certainly was not, and changed hands several more times. In July 1919, Grigorev, who had developed a hatred for "hook-nosed commissars," was murdered by another anarchist, Makhno, who was more amenable to the Bolsheviks.

Attempting to reinforce and control Makhno, the Politburo ordered Trotsky, traveling to the land of his birth in his armored train, to hold Odessa until "the last drop of blood." Trotsky did not interpret this to mean *his* blood, and he departed before the Whites retook the city on 23 August. The fate of Odessa was thereafter entangled with the Southern Army, the Ukrainian Directory, and the Polish Campaign, until the city was absorbed within Communist Ukraine in the summer of 1920.

Very early in the Russian conflict, Odessa experienced a serious shortage of money. An ad hoc "Committee for the Establishment of Credit" arranged for the local branch of Gosbank to issue "Small Change Bills of Odessa." One of

---

1   Both ship and stairs were named for Catherine's favorite general and lover.

Commie Currency

these, a *Desyatka* or 10-ruble note, is shown here. It has a passing similarity to the 1909 Tsarist bill, but the colors are flat and not so well aligned. The crowns have been removed from the eagle, which now looks rather Germanic, and, of course, there was no chance of exchanging this for gold.

Though dated 1917, these bills were printed from January to September 1918. Then it became necessary to discontinue the issue, as counterfeiters were flooding the city with fakes. The newspaper *Industrial Trade* informed its readers that 1000 rubles worth of these notes could be purchased on the street for 50 rubles (of a less suspect currency).[2] The legend at the head of the bill, "Counterfeiting forbidden by law," seems to have been an afterthought, as it was stamped onto the underlying design.

A visit to Odessa in October 2005 revealed that the city was once again a boomtown, her trolley tracks being torn up for shopping galleries. Though counterfeiting is no longer a major problem, vendors and scam artists are more active than elsewhere in Ukraine. Nor do beggars sit meekly by churches or near the underground as they do in Kiev. You can see them working the crowds of tourists at the Potemkin Steps, emptying their Styrofoam cups into bulging pockets every few minutes.

Several hundred miles north of Odessa, the city of Zhitomir also suffered from the Civil War money hunger. The city was occupied by Germans under Brest-Litovsk, but re-taken by the Soviets following the Armistice. Unlike Odessa, the Bolsheviks managed to keep this city, at least until the Polish Campaign, but it was a salient in a volatile frontline of the Civil War. Moscow had great difficulty in supplying bullets, let alone money, to this beachhead, so, following Odessa's lead, the locals printed their own.

One of these "Small Change Bills of the People's Bank of Zhitomir" is reproduced here. The denomination, 75 rubles, is unique in Russian or Soviet currency, so far as I know. The notes purported to be "guaranteed by State Credit Bills." Since those credit bills carried the absurd assertion that they were backed by gold, we have a case of a falsehood being warranted by a lie.

Even so, until the bills became completely worthless, entrepreneurs printed their own, including the usual warning "Counterfeiting Punishable by Law." Attempting counter-measures, the authorities pricked their bills in a pattern corresponding to the denomination. Visible when held to a strong light (but unfortunately impossible to reproduce here), the digits "75" are punched just left of the hand-stamped serial number. Either this bill is genuine, or a counterfeiter learned how to use a needle. Very soon, it became a moot point as price inflation overtook small change bills.

ON THE BLEEDING EDGE

The word *Ukraine* can be translated as edge, frontier, or borderland.[3] The country's name is tragically ironic, since Ukraine's history has not been the obscurity of the edge, but a repertoire of being caught in the middle.

---

2 12 September issue, in R.V. Nikolayev *Money, Time, Power* (St. Petersburg: Petersburg Collector, 2002), 40.

3 Until 1991, the region was referred to as *the* Ukraine, but after independence, the article was dropped. (There are no indefinite articles in Russian or Ukrainian, so this is an issue only for foreign writers.

Four: Main Enemy

The Vikings were sailing to Constantinople when they stopped to found the Kievan state. The Tatars were riding toward Western Europe when they found easy pickings in Ukraine. The Poles and the Russians contended over the region until Hetman Khmelnitsky signed Ukraine over to Tsar Alexei in 1654. Ukraine experienced no real independence during the Civil War, only chaos and interregna. True to form, the region served as battlefield for neighboring belligerents: Germany, Russia, and Poland. But there is one region of Ukraine that truly is on the edge, the Crimea, hanging like a diamond pendant over the Black Sea.

This is a rare 25-ruble "monetary token," issued by the short-lived "Provisional Government of the Crimean Region." The leaders of Crimea were inspired by the February Revolution, but disappointed in the October coup, and declared independence soon after, meeting in the old Palace of the Khans in Bakhchisarai. The Bolsheviks seized the nearby city of Simferopol and soon controlled the peninsula, but were overthrown in their turn by the Germans. The Kaiser's troops left in November 1918, and the Provisionals returned.

The head of that administration was Solomon Krym, a former Kadet (a socialist alternative to the Bolsheviks) and a Karaite, member of an ancient and exotic Judaic sect. He issued this bill (top left among the eight signatures at the foot). But the Bolsheviks turned up again in April 1919, and forced him from power. The Reds, in turn, fled from Denikin's army two months later, and the Whites then controlled the Crimea until the final chapter of the Civil War.

The political situation in the main body of Ukraine was even more chaotic; Kiev changed hands at least fifteen times. After declaring Ukrainian independence in November 1917, three successive administrations attempted to hold the new nation, clinging to one foreign patron or another in their attempts to beat the Reds. New currencies were introduced and replaced as quickly as the changing administrations. Price inflation forced the populace to use whatever money was to be had, including the many forgeries and knockoffs.

The new notes were issued as *Karbovanets*, a word probably derived in the same way as the Russian word ruble—from notches cut in silver bars used in ancient times for payment. Each Karbovanets was worth two *Griven*, the term for the silver bar.

Presented here are two 50-Karbovantsiv (plural form), first issued by the Central Rada in April 1918. Only one month earlier, the trident had been adopted as the state seal. This was a reference to the Ruriks, who founded Rus. Standing to each side on the bill, a peasant couple holds a shovel and sickle, symbols of Ukraine's rich earth. An inscription warns that "Forgery is Punishable by Imprisonment," alongside the State Bank Director's signature, Lebid Yurchik. The novelist Mikhail Bulgakov satirized the difficulties of dealing with the new money:

> Vasilisa's blue eyes glowered morosely. In the third bundle of ten bills there was one forgery, in the fourth— two, in the sixth— two, in the ninth three bills in succession were unmistakably of the kind for which Lebid-Yurchik threatened to imprison him…The peasant had a sort of gloomy look instead of being cheerful… and the paper was better than Lebid's. 'One of these will do for the cab fare tomorrow', said Vasilisa aloud to himself. 'And I've got to go down to the market,

Commie Currency

anyway. They don't look too hard at them there.[4]

The Rada was formed in November 1917, but was forced out of Kiev two months later by a small contingent of the Red Guard. They returned within weeks, but were again overthrown by a coup on 29 April. The Rada was replaced with a "Ukrainian People's Republic," led by Hetman Skoropadsky. The Republic introduced paper Griven in October 1918; this 10 Griven note was printed in Germany by the hetman's masters.

The Germans may have liked Skoropadsky, but few others did, and he departed very shortly after the Armistice. His currency continued to circulate, however, and in the meantime, the Rada more or less returned, albeit with a new name—the Ukrainian Directory. They declared war on the Soviets and managed to occupy Kiev on 16 January 1919. They could not hold the capital, however, and were forced out after just three weeks. Retreating westward by stages, the Directory eventually fetched up in Kamenets-Podolsk, where they grew irrelevant and finally expired in June 1920.

The Directory churned out piles of money to pay for their war against the Reds, and produced the most attractive of all Ukrainian Civil War currency. With the 1000-Karbovantsiv note, all the warnings, warranties, and signatures (still Lebid Yurchik!) have been moved to the reverse. Only the denomination and portraiture remain on the obverse, featuring attractive figures holding the mace and cornucopia, the symbols of state and plenitude. Production of these bills followed the Directory, being printed first in Kiev, then Kamenets-Podolsk, and finally in Warsaw. The Polish artistic influence is obvious.

After the Directory was forced from Kiev, the Bolsheviks seemed triumphant, but the summer of 1919 witnessed the White Guard's greatest victories. Breaking out of the Crimea, and advancing westward from the Donbas, the Volunteer Army seized Kiev on 23 August and Odessa on the same day. The situation stabilized for a few months, and then a new player entered the game.

In early 1920, Poland decided to seize lands to which she claimed historical presence. Moving east with surprising ease, Polish troops captured the capital city in June. Denikin blamed the Poles for "saving" the Bolsheviks,[5] and with some justification. But by then, the Whites were already on the retreat across a broader front, southward to their final stronghold. An attack by Moscow met stiff resistance from the Poles and stalled at the Vistula River. In March 1921, Russia was forced to cede a large part of Ukraine to Poland. The rest of Ukraine became a Soviet Republic, and Ukrainian aspirations were lost, for seven long decades.

You may have noticed that the two examples of the 50-Karbovantsiv note differ slightly, by the shade of ink used. They were both printed in Odessa, but by opposing parties. The one marked AO 204 was issued by the Rada, early in 1919. When the Bolsheviks re-captured the city, they found the plates and dashed off forty or fifty million of the notes, starting with the serial AO 236. Using a standard trick, the Soviets printed currency designed by their enemies, and then declared the money invalid after spending it.

---

4 Mikhail Bulgakov, *The White Guard,* trans. Michael Glenny (Chicago: Academy Chicago, 2000), 39.

5 Evan Mawdsley, *The Russian Civil War* (Edinburgh, Scotland: Birlinn, 2000), 205.

Four: Main Enemy

SIBERIAN CIRCUS

European and Asiatic Russia are separated by a north-south range of marginal mountains: the Urals. From there, it is 3500 miles via rail to Russia's port on the Pacific, Vladivostok. In the summer of 1918, this vital link was controlled by the misinformed and badly treated Czech Legion. Though they were mainly trying to get home, the Czechs blocked the Bolsheviks from Siberia, and thereby empowered the various other forces there. Whites and warlords, patriots and scoundrels, Brits, Americans, and Japanese, turned the vastness of Siberia into a multi-ring circus. Sited along the trans-Siberian railroad, these regional capitals suffered the worst of the eastern conflict: Omsk, 500 miles east of the Urals; Irkutsk, west of Lake Baikal; Chita, in the Transbaikal region; and Vladivostok, capital of the Primorskaya.

The Bolsheviks enjoyed little initial support in Siberia—a region of many small landowners and few intellectuals—and received less than ten percent of the Constituent Assembly votes cast there. A provisional, left-leaning government was formed in Omsk, in the autumn of 1918, but within weeks, a former Tsarist admiral named Kolchak led a conservative coup.

Alexander Kolchak was a moody but high-minded individual, and his rule was fraught with ironies, contradictions that contributed to his ultimate defeat. He was an admiral without a ship, commanding a force thousands of miles from the sea. As he had little experience with land warfare, his offensive in the spring of 1919 faltered and fell back.

He ruled by fiat, while insisting he only served as caretaker for a future democratic government. However, he never found the time to establish a functional civilian administration, causing his support to trickle away.

The British supplied his army with abundant weaponry, but so much of this made its way to the Reds that Trotsky sent a thank-you note to General Knox. Kolchak also had at his disposal literally tons of gold, even as he issued paper currency, and this final irony led the admiral to his death.

Using a tactic tested elsewhere, the Bolsheviks attempted to undermine Kolchak's rule by flooding the rebellious territory with Kerenki. The Reds printed as many as 140 million rubles a day, being joined in this frenzy of ink by assorted counterfeiters. Out of 90 billion rubles in circulation, an estimated 80 billion were the easily reproduced Kerenki.[6] The Omsk administration had to confront this problem.

The problem was not a lack of valuables. The Imperial reserves of gold and silver, stored at Kazan, had been captured by the Czech Legion in 1918. Kolchak assumed control of the 36 railway cars, loaded with 775 tons of gold and 540 tons of silver. Declining to use this bounty for expenses, the admiral instead ordered the preparation of "Short-Term Bonds of the State Treasury." Issued with a term of one year, the bonds promised five percent interest and redemption by the All-Russian government intended to succeed Kolchak's rule. This example shown here (reduced by five percent) is in the amount of 500 rubles and carries a maturity date of 1 July 1920. Unfortunately, due to shortages of proper paper and trained personnel, the bonds were only slightly more difficult to duplicate than the Kerenki they were intended to replace. All too soon, fake *Siberski* flooded the market, and their value plummeted.

---

6   Nikolayev, 58.

Commie Currency

The admiral himself did not outlive his bonds. In November 1919, the Reds recaptured Omsk and the All-Russian Army retreated to Irkutsk. Kolchak remained with the slow-moving gold train, along with members of the Czech Legion. Towards the end of January 1920, the Czechs traded both the gold and the admiral for passage to the seacoast. Fearing the loss of their prisoner in the volatile war zone, the Reds quickly decided to shoot Kolchak, and shoved his body through a hastily chopped hole through the ice in the closest river. Far from his beloved ocean, Admiral Kolchak found a watery grave.

Moving east 2000 miles and back 17 months, the port of Vladivostok had just welcomed the arrival of the Allies. The first Americans landed in August 1918, joining some 1200 British, a few French, and a large contingent of Japanese (see below). General William Graves arrived with the rest of his infantry, totaling 8117 men, in September, having been warned by the Secretary of War that he "would be walking on eggs filled with dynamite."

President Woodrow Wilson had authorized a 'humanitarian' mission, to help transport the Czech Legion to the killing fields of France. But the Czechs decided to fight the Reds. General Graves struggled to maintain neutrality while bringing some semblance of order to chaotic Siberia, all the time skirmishing with both the Whites and the Reds. In April 1920, the Americans left, marking the end of US "intervention"; the Czechs departed six months later.

Meanwhile, the Zemstva was searching for some way to improve their finances. In an unguarded warehouse, they discovered an unused and unfamiliar currency, totaling three and a half billion rubles, in denominations of 25 and 100-ruble notes. One example of these beautifully executed bills is shown here, and depicts Ceres holding a sickle and surrounded by her fruits.

This note has a shared history with the 200-ruble bond in chapter five. Bills and bonds both were prepared for the Kerensky administration, which collapsed before they could be delivered. The bonds were shipped to the provisional government in Omsk, which also fell before they could be delivered. The bills languished in Vladivostok, until the locals found and issued them, in June 1920.

Naturally, the currency was called *Amerikansky*. Although this currency is obviously quite difficult to forge, the value of the bills began to decline from the first moment of use; by October, they were worthless. Popular rejection of the Amerikansky may have something to do with the transience of the American troops. The Yanks had been welcomed with parades and feasts on their arrival; when they left, a dockside band played "Hard Times Come Again No More."[7]

The largest foreign army to be stationed in Russia during the civil war belonged to Japan, eventually totaling more than 70,000. Their troops landed in Vladivostok ahead of the Americans, spread throughout the Primorskaya, and extended their influence as far as Lake Baikal. As one of the Allies, Japan was theoretically involved in stabilizing the East and encouraging Russia to return to the European war. In reality, Japan preferred chaos in Siberia, which would facilitate the construction of a Japanese sphere of influence. To this end, Japan chose as its proxy one of the most capricious and hot-tempered figures of the period: Grigory Mikhailovitch Semenov.

---

[7] Richard O'Conner, "Yanks in Siberia," *American Heritage Magazine*, August 1974.

Four: Main Enemy

Semenov was a native of Transbaikal who served in World War I, and returned to Chita as regional commissar for the Kerensky administration. The Siberian Provisional Government appointed him as military commander for the area, with the rank of Lieutenant General. Kolchak only reluctantly agreed to the posting, but Semenov was enthusiastically supported by the Japanese, who paid him a lavish stipend. Semenov's other source of revenue derived from Chita's location on the Trans-Siberian Railroad, the only means of transporting men and supplies from Vladivostok to the front. In brief, the Lieutenant General extorted a portion of every trainload that passed through his fiefdom.

In early 1919, Semenov declared himself "Ataman of the Transbaikal Cossacks," and ruled as a Cossack cliché. Using an armored train called *Destroyer*, the Ataman traveled from one helpless village to another, stealing, killing, raping, and burning as the mood took him. A cocaine addict, Semenov once "allowed a subordinate to shoot ten boxcars full of prisoners just to show that 'shootings can be carried out on Sunday as well as any other day'."[8] This banditry, practiced in the cause of anti-Bolshevism, went a long way towards discrediting the Whites and ensuring their eventual loss.

The problems Semenov gave his presumed allies also contributed to Red victory. In October 1919, the Ataman stopped a train loaded with American weapons being sent to Omsk and demanded fifteen thousand rifles. Even when threatened with a massacre, Lieutenant Ryan and his 50 soldiers refused to submit. On this occasion, the Ataman backed down, but the next January, one of his subordinates attacked an American detachment guarding a railway station. Although they had only rifles and grenades against the cannon and machine-guns carried on the *Destroyer*, the Americans forced the armored train's retreat and surrender.

One of the trains upon which Semenov extracted his 'toll' carried watermarked paper, sent from America for the government in Omsk. After the death of Kolchak, Semenov renamed his territory the "Russian Eastern Border," and decided to print his own currency from the purloined paper. (Perhaps the 150,000-dollar monthly salary from the Japanese was insufficient.) Denominations of 100 and 500 rubles were printed; they were called *Sparrows* and *Doves*, in reference to the crudely drawn eagles on the obverse. One of the Sparrows is shown here, and gives the appearance of having been printed using a woodblock. The heavy black ink used has bled through each side.

In just six months, Ataman Semenov printed a lot of these little birds: 1.2 billion rubles in Sparrows and 8.6 billion rubles worth of Doves. By July 1920, one ruble of the Ataman's money had a purchasing power of just one-half of a kopeck. Soon, they were exchanged by weight rather than face value. On 22 October, a local newspaper called *Kazakh Echo* reported, "in the Manchurian [railway] station, the 'donation' of one dollar would secure two pounds of Chitinsky bills."[9] On the same day this article was published, Chita fell to the Bolsheviks, and the Ataman flew away to Manchuria. He continued to work with the Japanese, until the Soviet Union invaded Manchuria near the end of WWII. Grigory Semenov was captured, put on trial, and executed by hanging in August 1946.

---

8   Benson Bobrick, *East of the Sun* (New York: Poseidon Press, 1992), 404.

9   Nikolaev, 76.

Commie Currency

Chita's position on the Trans-Siberian Railroad, and the difficulty of moving goods through Semenov's fiefdom, gave the city a nickname, "the cork." A cork of a different kind was controlled by a Red Army partisan whose crimes rivaled those of Grigory Semenov.

Jacob Tryapitsin was born in 1897 into a family of craftsmen. Known for his physical strength, Jacob enlisted early for the Great War and, through his boldness, earned a command. He survived the war, though he afterwards walked with a limp, and returned to Russian as a fanatical Bolshevik. Tryapitsin joined the partisans in the Primorskaya and soon commanded his own detachment.

His forces attacked Nikolayevsk-on-the-Amur, capturing the city on 29 February 1920. Nikolayevsk is located opposite Sakhalin Island, and controls access from eastern Siberia to the Sea of Japan and the Pacific. Although the city had declined in importance since the opening of Vladivostok, still the site was useful to the Japanese, who had a garrison there.

Nikolayevsk was prosperous, with an estimated net worth of over 50 million pre-war gold rubles. After its "liberation," the town fathers formed a Provisional Soviet, but actual power resided in the hands of the "lame dictator," as Tryapitsin was known, and his chief of staff.

This was Jacob's 22 year-old girlfriend, Nina Lebedeva, politically an SR, who enjoyed horse riding, guns, and red leather. Together, they ruled Nikolayevsk like the Queen of Hearts ruled Wonderland, but instead of "Off with their heads!" it was "Up against the wall!" As for the Japanese garrison, Tryapitsin and Major Isikava signed an accord of cooperation, but relations quickly deteriorated. On 25 March, Japanese soldiers and civilians were all murdered, and most of the town was burned.

Expecting retaliation, the lame dictator desperately needed ammunition, and sought to obtain it by the only means readily available, on the black market. A local newspaper, *The Appeal*, reported that the going rate was 10 rounds per ruble.[10] But where would the money come from? The Provisional Soviet, no doubt at the prodding of the lame dictator, authorized an issue of bonds in denominations of 250 to 1000 rubles.

One example of these amusingly crude bonds is on display. The off-center placement of the printing shows that the bond was cut from the lower right corner of a large sheet. The local State Bank has stamped the bill with an old seal depicting the Romanov double-headed eagle. This stamp partially obliterates the dubious claim that the bonds should be accepted as equal to State Credit Bills.

The bonds were designed by a provincial art-school teacher, who made what the newspaper called an "annoying blunder." In 1920, the nation ruled by Lenin was called the "Russian Federation of Soviet Republics," abbreviated in Cyrillic as РФСР. But, by mistake, the schoolteacher put РСФР at the top of his bills, though it is correct in the background lettering in the center of the note. (The error was fixed on the 500 and 1000-ruble bonds.)

Whether misspelled or not, the bonds did not long circulate; they were issued in May 1920, and before the month ended, Jacob and Nina were on the run. Arrested by Bolshevik authorities, they were put on trial for ordering mass executions, of the Japanese and many others. Tryapitsin's defense was not to deny any of his actions, but to claim that such excesses were entirely reasonable in the name of the Revolution. Although this is the same justification used by

---

10   Nikolayev, 62.

Four: Main Enemy

Lenin, Trotsky, and Stalin, still the court found the defendants guilty and sentenced the dictator and his mistress to (what else?) the firing squad. It is said that, with his dying breath, Jacob Tryapitsin turned to Nina Lebedeva and whispered: "I am only sorry for you; as for the rest, to hell with it."[11]

Perhaps the Bolsheviks were trying to mollify Japan by shooting Tryapitsin, but the Japanese used his brutality as justification for a larger presence in Siberia, from 70,000 to 200,000 men. Anti-Bolshevik resistance sputtered out after the fall of Chita, but parts of Siberia continued to be shared between the Reds and the Rising Sun for two more years. In this atmosphere, a buffer state was thought desirable, for which purpose Moscow created the "Far Eastern Republic."

Although it was originally proposed by the SR-Menshevik coalition as a truly independent entity, the Bolsheviks adapted the concept as a puppet. Serving as a polite fiction, the FER nevertheless issued currency, such as this 1000-ruble bill. On the reverse, a bucolic Siberia is depicted. A peasant in traditional costume uses a stone to sharpen his sickle; in the background, the fruits of his labor stand under the gentle sun. This is an idealization of a land nearly obliterated by the Civil War; worse soon followed with collectivization and the Gulag.

The Japanese finally withdrew in October 1922; Vladivostok fell on the 25th, and being no longer needed, the FER was absorbed into the Soviet Union on 14 November. The few remaining Whites fled to China, Manchuria, or elsewhere, and technically, this marked the end of the Russian Civil War. In reality, significant military struggle ended where it began in 1905, and where, curiously, Communism would collapse, seven decades further on. For the culminating act of this Russian tragedy, we return to the Crimea.

ONE AND UNDIVIDED

The principal leaders in the anti-Bolshevik struggle were Admiral Alexander Kolchak, General Anton Denikin, and General Baron Peter Wrangel. Kolchak was the commander-in-chief and the only one of the three not to survive the Civil War.

It is curious to note that the C-in-C's headquarters, in Omsk, were far removed from Kolchak's subordinates, and, for that matter, from the outside world. Even when the railway was clear, it took four to six weeks to reach Omsk with men, material, or messages. It was thus difficult for Kolchak to coordinate with subordinates Denikin and Wrangel.

Generals Denikin and Wrangel were, successively, commanders of the White Army in South Russia. Situated much closer to the water than the landlocked admiral, the generals could be supplied via the Black Sea; when the unhappy end arrived, they escaped the same way.

After the Volunteers and Cossack fighters were forced to retreat south to the Kuban, they settled in a more strategically advantageous position, with the Caucasus Mountains at their back. In addition, the Whites enjoyed a higher degree of local support in the Kuban. These advantages were vital, since the Red Army heavily outnumbered the anti-Bolsheviks, 80,000 to 9,000 at first. More Red troops poured in as the fighting intensified.

General Denikin's men proved to be remarkable fighters, defeating the much larger Red 12th Army. The Communist Central Committee then declared the Southern Front to be the most

---

11   Nikolayev, 63.

Commie Currency

critical, proclaiming: "Red Terror is now essential." Bolshevik successes against the Cossacks, a separate force from the Southern Army, led Lenin to expect final victory by summer, 1919.

Once again, he was mistaken. In an action known as the "Moscow Directive," the Whites advanced across a front so broad that Denikin was forced to use smaller-scale maps to follow the action. Along the Dnieper, the Don, and the Volga, the Whites moved upriver.

October of 1919 recorded the high-water mark of the anti-Bolshevik advance on Moscow, with the capture of Orel, only 240 miles from the capital. Denikin estimated that his forces controlled 350,000 square miles, on which lived 42 million people.[12]

The problem was that only a few of those millions were convinced of the White cause. If Moscow had witnessed popular uprisings, if Bolshevik supporters had lost heart, then Lenin's government would have fallen. These things did not happen, and the turn-about was shockingly sudden. In less than two months, the White Army lost all that it had gained, and retreated beyond the Don. With these reversals, the Cossacks and the Southern Army had a falling-out, and foreign support faded away. In March 1920, the remnants of Denikin's army crossed over to the Crimea, and the general resigned, departing to Constantinople and exile.

Denikin's successor was Peter Wrangel, and he understood well his predicament, recognizing that his goal would be to extricate the Volunteers and anti-Bolshevik officers, not to defeat the Reds. Geography favored the new commander, since the Crimean peninsula is practically an island, and Moscow was temporarily distracted by the Polish War. But a Soviet-Polish armistice was signed on 12 October, and the final Red attack began two weeks later. General Wrangel successfully carried out his final tasks, fighting a rear-guard action as the ships were loaded. He himself was among the last to depart, leaving Sevastopol on 14 November 1920. As the last significant group of resisters steamed south, the Bolsheviks could construct, as Lenin had promised two years earlier, the "socialist order."

These are examples of currency issued by General Denikin and General Baron Wrangel. The first is a 200-ruble bill issued in 1919, at the height of Denikin's advance. Beneath the Cross of St. George is a depiction of a Moscow statue of General Mikhail Skobelev, with the Kremlin in the background. This monument, like the statue of Pushkin and Taganka Square, was a site for soapbox orators and argumentation.

> Gradually the meetings in the various parts of Moscow assumed each its specific character. At the Skobelev Monument, the speakers were usually representatives of the various parties, from Cadets and Populist-Socialists to Bolsheviks. Here the speeches were violent, but to the point. No one was allowed to talk hot air in front of Skobelev. The moment anyone began, the crowd shouted in unison: 'Off with you to the Taganka! Out you go!' In Taganka Square you could indeed say anything you liked - for instance that Kerensky was an apostate from the village of Shpola.[13]

---

12   Mawdsley, 213

13   Konstantin Paustovsky, *In That Dawn*, trans. Manya Harari and Andrew Thomson, (Moscow: Progress Publishers, 1967), 3.

Four: Main Enemy

A cavalry commander and hero of the Turkish War of 1877, Skobelev always rode a white charger; naturally, he was known as the "White General." In later years, he was an ardent Russian nationalist who warned of a coming conflict between his empire and that of the Germans. His prescience and his nickname made General Skobelev very popular with the White Guard.

The 200-ruble note is quite worn; it was heavily used during the "Moscow Directive," but the last note illustrating this chapter appears not to have circulated. In fact, this 10,000-ruble note was issued in the final days of the anti-Bolshevik struggle. The designer has reverted to the use of allegorical figures, similar to the portraits of Minerva and Athena on the Rostov note in the previous frame. Here, the figure on the left is the *tyche* of St. Petersburg, identified by the Church of St. Paul in that city's fortress, while the other figure sits before the Kremlin's Saviour Tower and represents Moscow. Together, they emphasize the slogan of the Southern Army, which is printed around and above: "United and Indivisible Russia."

Why did the White Guard lose? In part, the tragic outcome was, like comedy, a matter of timing. At first, when the Bolsheviks were few and could have been easily toppled, their opponents were ambivalent and the Allies were only focused on the war in Europe. By the time opinion began to harden against the Reds, they had consolidated their control of many power structures. Battlefield action was also timed poorly for the Whites and luckily for the Reds. For example, when Denikin's forces made their advance in the summer of 1919, Kolchak was already a spent shell.

A more important factor might be called "centering." Moscow occupied the central position, with rail and river running from there. The Bolsheviks were able to make good use of their location, and move men and material where needed. Coupled with the issue of timing, this allowed the Communists to act as firemen, racing from one hot spot to the next. Winston Churchill reflected on the importance of logistics, drawing on the insect world for comparison:

> The ancient capital lay at the centre of a web of railroads radiating to every point of the compass. And in the midst a spider! Vain hope to crush the spider by the advance of lines of encircling flies![14]

Perhaps the most vital factor in the Russian Civil War was that, like the void at the center of a wheel (an old Zen parable), the Reds held steady while their opponents whirled around. Lenin, Trotsky, *et al*, always knew exactly what they wanted; to stay in power and to hold as much of the Russian Empire as was practical.

The Bolsheviks were politicians of the pragmatic and the promise. They trumpeted slogans made of the most blatant lies, and they were never hampered by any sense of tradition or fair play. Though obvious extremists, the Bolsheviks successfully packaged themselves as centrists, depicting their critics as left or right "deviationists." They also offered autonomy to various nationalities, intending to seize back the land as soon as possible.

The Whites, on the other hand, were a mixed bag of aspirations and conflicts. Some had visions of restoring the Russian Empire, though few actually wanted to bring back the tsar. Others fought for ethnic identity or full independence. Many people dreamed of some kind

---

14 Winston Churchill, *The Aftermath*, (New York: Charles Scribner's Sons, 1929), 242-243.

Commie Currency

of Left alternative, ranging from mild socialism to wild anarchism. The Bolsheviks were adroit in exploiting the divisions among their adversaries; Divide and Conquer brought them success in the Civil War.

What of the intervention by foreign powers: how did this affect the outcome of the war? Following the February Revolution, and even after the October Coup, the concern of the Allies was to somehow persuade Russia to reenter the war in Europe. Only after the Bolsheviks had permitted Germany to overrun one-fourth of the former empire, did London and Paris reluctantly conclude that Moscow would never take up arms again in that conflict. (They placed their hopes on America instead.)

When the Great War ended, an atmosphere of mutual distrust and hostility existed between the Soviets and the Allies, but many in the West nursed sympathies for the aims of socialism. The lines of communication, of diplomats and intelligence agents, were strained, tenuous, and often twisted by prejudice. So, ambivalence and ambiguity reigned. Trotsky complained to London's unofficial ambassador to Moscow: " [Prime Minister] Lloyd George is like a man playing roulette and scattering chips on every number."[15]

Extending this analogy of gambling to the other powers, we may say that Germany played successfully against an incompetent house, but was eventually forced to retire. France placed a few chips but snatched them away when threatened with their loss. America disapproved of the game, and took part reluctantly, only to assist the other gamblers. Finally, Japan played the longest and most successfully, withdrawing when the stakes were no longer worth the playing.

The foreign powers were, following the severe toll of the Great War, understandably reluctant to provide the men necessary to effect regime change in Bolshevik Russia. If there is a lesson, it must be that half-hearted measures never succeed. The Allies' intervention in the Russian Civil War did little but prolong the conflict, consolidate the Soviets' control, and facilitate the rise of Stalin.

---

15 Bruce Lockhart, *Memoirs of a British Agent*, (New York: Pan Books, 2002), 231.

Four: Main Enemy

Commie Currency

Four: Main Enemy

Commie Currency

Four: Main Enemy

Commie Currency

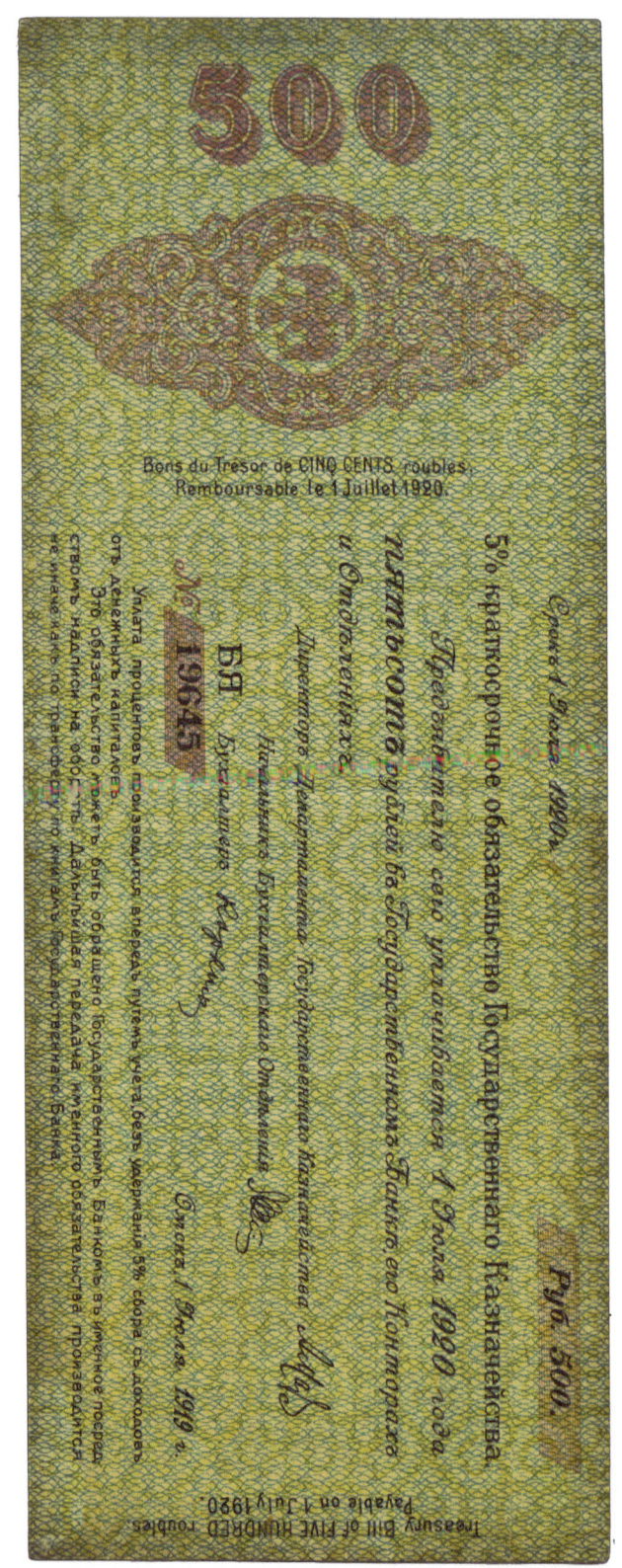

Four: Main Enemy

Commie Currency

Four: Main Enemy

Commie Currency

Four: Main Enemy

Five: Promises, Promises

In normal circumstances, government bonds provide funds for capital improvements or extraordinary expenses. When properly administered, these obligations enhance revenue while avoiding tax increases and inflation, at least in the short run. However, potential purchasers of these instruments want to have confidence in the issuing authority's ability and willingness to repay, and in the stability of their currency. The record of Russian bonds in the 20th century, unhappily, is a tale of misplaced confidence, hysterical wistfulness, and blatant theft.

DEAD FIVER

In the final decade of the 19th century, Russia turned away from Germany and aligned with France. Under the terms of the Franco-Russian Military Convention of 1894, the French Republic underwrote obligations for the Russian monarchy. This is a 100-ruble bond issued by Nicholas II in June 1908.[1] It paid five percent interest (hence the name *Fivers*) and had a maturity date of 1 March 1917. In December 1996, the Russian weekly *Arguments and Facts* carried an article written by Ivan Roslyakov describing the history of these bonds, from which the following is adapted.

Russian bonds paid as much as 14% at a time when interest elsewhere ran less than 3%. Due to the attractiveness of this investment, fully a tenth of the population of France owned Russian bonds when war broke out in 1914. In that year, some 200 million rubles were paid out as interest.

This bond was sold in 1908, and matured on the first of March 1917. But Nicholas abdicated one day later, and the holder did not collect. The following February, the All-Russia Central Executive Committee made it official— the obligations of the Imperial Government would not be met.

The loss to bondholders in France was enormous, amounting to five billion gold francs or four billion (1996) dollars. More than 100,000 French families lost all or much of their savings and French newspapers reported waves of resulting suicides from 1918 to 1920. The loss of so much capital contributed in no small part to the French post-was economic downturn. It may have exacerbated the demand for war payments from Germany and inadvertently encouraged the rise of Hitler.

In 1921, there was a "hint" that some payment might, after all, be forthcoming and in 1927, the French government made an attractive offer to the Soviets. France would invest new sums in Russia in return for payment on the old debts. The Russian ambassador, Rakovsky by name, signed off on this but Stalin refused to agree and Rakovsky, for his troubles, was shot.

In 1992, Russian President Boris Yeltsin indicated his willingness to discuss the matter of these bonds, and in November of 1995, an agreement was signed by the Russian Prime Minister Chernomyrdin. In settlement, 400 million dollars was to be paid to the French government, ten cents on the dollar. Many in Russia argued that this agreement would set a very bad precedent; imagine if compensation were to be paid to the descendants of all whose property was seized by the Bolsheviks. That argument proved moot; as of March 2010, no payments had been made.

---

1 Size reduced by 50%.

Commie Currency

GIVE ME LIBERTY (AND RUBLES)

Our next bond is a type known as the "Liberty Loan," intended by the Provisional government to pay for war materials.[2] It illustrates that administration's fatal misunderstanding in regard to the people's wish for peace. The rhetoric reveals how the Provisional Ministers saw themselves, and unknowingly predicts the consequences of their failure.

Now, selling bonds is not inherently inflationary; money is simply being reallocated. However, both the Tsarist and the Provisional governments allowed banks to exchange cash for securities and to accept them as collateral. This contributed to the growing rate of price rises, which exceeded 300% in the eight months Kerensky was in office. It had taken the Imperial government four times as long to generate that level of price inflation.

The Liberty Loan was first sold just 25 days after the Tsar's abdication. That date is at the bottom of the example shown here, along with its place of issue, the capital, Petrograd. (In a flush of wartime patriotism, the capital had been renamed; Petersburg sounded too German.) Above a depiction of the Duma in an oval frame are the words "Loan of Liberty," and below that the rate of interest and the amount (40 rubles at 5%).

The first signature is that of the Prime Minister, Lvov, next to his printed title. He has actually signed himself "Prince Lvov." Use of his title gave offense to many in the Duma and among the people. Some asked, "Have we gotten rid of a tsar, only to be stuck with a prince?"

Lvov's future replacement has signed at the very bottom, "Minister of Justice- A. Kerensky."

Various other ministers have also signed this document. It would be reminiscent of the Declaration of Independence, except that, in this case, the signers are asking for the pledge of others:

> To you, citizen of a great and free Russia, who holds dear our future Motherland, we address our fervent appeal. The powerful enemy has deeply encroached on our boundaries and threatened to overcome us.... Only an effort of all our strength can secure for us our desired victory. We need to spend many billions, to save our country and to complete the construction of free Russia on the basis of equality and truth. We lend the money of the State, investing in new bonds, to save from ruin our freedom and property.

By "the powerful enemy" the ministers meant Germany. But the deadly enemy of a "free Russia" was closer at hand. Obsessed with the Kaiser, Kerensky failed to preserve Russian freedom and property from the Communists.

The President of the Free Economic Society called on everyone "to give his savings for the great cause of freedom."[3] The people responded with their rubles, at first. But as casualties worsened throughout the summer, they listened to the Bolsheviks and turned away from the war in disgust. As a result, the sale of Liberty Loans fell precipitously—from 33 million rubles in March to less than 3 million in September.[4]

---

2 Size reduced by 10%.

3 N. V. Chaikovsky, in Orlando Figes, *A People's Tragedy*, (New York: Viking, 1997), 412.

4 Paul N. Apostol, "Credit Operations," in *Russian Public Finance During the War* (New Haven, CT: Yale University Press, 1928), 275.

Five: Promises, Promises

Ironically, after taking power the Bolsheviks continued to produce Liberty Loans, but issued them as currency, without borrowing the money beforehand. They called this "Surrogate Money."[5]

WAR CREDIT

War is hell—to pay for. Imperial Russia purchased much-needed war material from France, Britain, and the United States, but the carnage of the World War soon outstripped the country's ability to pay. A financial conference was held in London in February 1915, and Russia received a loan of £100,000,000. France was to bear half the costs of this aid.

That money was soon exhausted, and a second conference in September 1915 authorized twenty-five million pounds a month, to be paid to Russia over a year's time. Every six months after that, a new meeting kept the money flowing to Russia, and kept Russian peasants flowing to the slaughter.

A portion of the credit—from Britain, France, and, in 1917, the United States—was allocated "to the needs of Russian commerce," without Allied oversight, as was the case for war material. The method used for commercial support was "special credit… by the Bank of England to facilitate the discount of bills drawn by Russian banks and endorsed by the Russian State Bank."[6]

After the February Revolution, many of the well-off in Russia began to move their wealth abroad. The ruble declined dramatically against foreign currencies; trying to stem the flood, the Provisional Administration, on 5 June, forbade the transfer of rubles abroad. The American consul in Petrograd reported on the situation:

> The Russian public, more moved by the approaching panic than by patriotism [here referring to the failure of the "Liberty Loan"], are striving by fair means or foul to liquidate their holdings in Russia and transfer the proceeds into foreign security or values. Money has been sent out of the country by every conceivable means, and speculation [arbitrage] made possible by the differences between the official Russian rate of exchange and the open commercial rate has run riot.[7]

The best means of moving wealth abroad, for Russians with the right connections, were bills of exchange, as authorized by the war conferences and administered by the Banks of England and Russia. One example is shown here.[8]

This bill of exchange was purchased on 12/25 August 1917 (the difference in dates comes from the Julian calendar used by the Russians until 1918) at the Azoff-Don Commercial Bank. What was exchanged for it is unknown—probably, heavily discounted treasury securities. The London conference had set the discount rate at seven percent, but that would have been after any discount taken within Russia.

---

5   L.N. Zaitseva, *State Paper Money of RSFSR and USSR* (Moscow: Mezhnumizmatika, 1989), 37.

6   Memorandum from Russian Ministers of Foreign Affairs (Tereshchenko) and Finance (Shingarev), in Robert Paul Browder and Aleksandr Fyodorovich Kerensky, *The Russian Provisional Government, 1917: documents, volume 1* (Stanford, CA: Stanford University Press, 1961), 503-504.

---

7   North Winship, "Report to the Department of State, 19 June 1917," in Browder and Kerensky, 510.

8   Size reduced by 25%, second page not shown.

Commie Currency

A few days later, the bill was entered into the Baring Brothers account at the Russian State Bank. Messrs. Baring Brothers handled all such exchanges, under a contract made in February 1915.[9] From there, it made its way through Credit Lyonnais, agent for the Russian government in France, and eventually to Latham & Co. in London. In October, it was accepted by the Bank of England, and on 21 January 1918, the sum of £5,000 was paid, with His Majesty's Government taking two pounds, one shilling, for the tax stamp.

In July 1917, Tereshchenko and Shingarev had complained, "all our sums in British currency had been exhausted." Not so, the British ambassador assured them, "approximately 65 million pounds is still available."[10] This bill was drawn shortly after that, and accepted by the Bank of England in October—three weeks before the Bolsheviks seized power, and the flow of foreign credit ceased. It is an example of extraordinarily good timing, or luck, on the part of someone.

ADOPT A BOND

In mid-October 1917, representatives of the Provisional Government who were in America signed a contract with the American Banknote Company to print bonds. They were to be prepared in five categories, identical except for the background colors, with 2 million issued in each category. The face value was to be 200 rubles apiece, with 20 coupons of 4.5 rubles each paid out over a ten-year span to maturity. The total issue then was to be 10 million bonds, valued at 2 billion rubles. Before they could be printed, however, the Kerensky government fell.

Preparations for printing the bonds had advanced to the point that it would have cost as much to cancel as to go forward, so in January 1918 the first category was finished. Most likely, American taxpayers paid for the printing. Some $325,000,000 in cash or credit had already been "advanced" to Russia by November 1917, with much of that going to American contractors who "have been manufacturing munitions, clothing… and various equipment for the Russian Government."[11]

It was decided to send all 10 million bonds to Siberia to prop up the provisional government there. They arrived in Vladivostok in April on board a civilian steamer, the *Santa Cruz*, and stayed in storage until September of the next year. All parties involved quarreled over their proper use, but the bonds were finally sent to Omsk, arriving just before that city fell to the Red Army in November 1919.

Back onto the train went these bonds, along with Kolchak, the Czech Legion, and the tsarist gold reserves that the Czechs had picked up earlier. In Irkutsk, the left-wing (but not exclusively Bolshevik) Soviet passed a statute regarding these bonds on 20 November 1919. This local council was responding to a severe shortage of money. Tsarist bills and Dumki circulated freely, but Kolchak had forbidden the use of the easily counterfeited Kerenki. And so, some of the crates were finally opened, the coupons were separated from the bonds, and both bonds and coupons from the first three categories were issued as currency.

They were immediately accepted, since the high artistic quality of this American paper could not be duplicated. The coupons enjoyed

---

9 Apostol, 310.

10 Browder and Kerensky, 505, 507.

11 "We Assist Russia; She Stays In War," *New York Times*, 3 November 1917, 3.

Five: Promises, Promises

a premium and were valued at five rubles in Siberski (chapter 4). But by early March, the Reds controlled central Siberia and invalidated all "White Guard" currency. Of course, this brought on renewed "money hunger." Finding the remaining bonds from categories four and five, the Bolsheviks stamped them and issued them as currency throughout the spring of 1920.

Presented here is an example of these "American Money-Bonds," from the fifth and final category—one of the last to be produced and used. This piece of paper was printed in the USA, traveled by steamship across the Pacific, and then sat in storage for a year and a half. It rode the rails several thousand miles to the Urals, returned halfway, and went back into storage. Finally, some anonymous Communist bureaucrat disfigured it with a hideous stamp and deigned to let it be used.

The stamp says, "It is compulsory to circulate this as equal to credit bills and accounting tokens of the Russian Socialist Federation of Soviet Republics." On the right side it adds, "Counterfeiting is a crime under the law." The irony, that the Bolsheviks would forbid others to duplicate what they themselves had stolen, was no doubt lost on them.

The image at top was, you will note, copyright by the American Banknote Company. Although I do not know for certain, it seems to me that the figures represent Mother Russia protecting the newly born Free Russia. This interpretation would also have been wasted on Russia's new rulers.

Also shown here is a coupon; this one is from the fourth category. If the bonds had been issued as originally planned by Kerensky, then this coupon would have been redeemed for cash on or after 16 October 1919, in payment of interest. Instead, on that date it was probably on the Siberian railway, being shuttled back and forth until it was finally 'adopted' by the Reds.

After the Bolsheviks consolidated their power on the country, and renamed it the Soviet Union, they began to issue their own bonds. This was done to help finance their grandiose five-year plans, but as we shall see in chapter seven, the Reds were no better than the Whites at paying their debts. First, however, we will consider the dizzying heights of hyperinflation in the nineteen-twenties.

Five: Promises, Promises

Commie Currency

Five: Promises, Promises

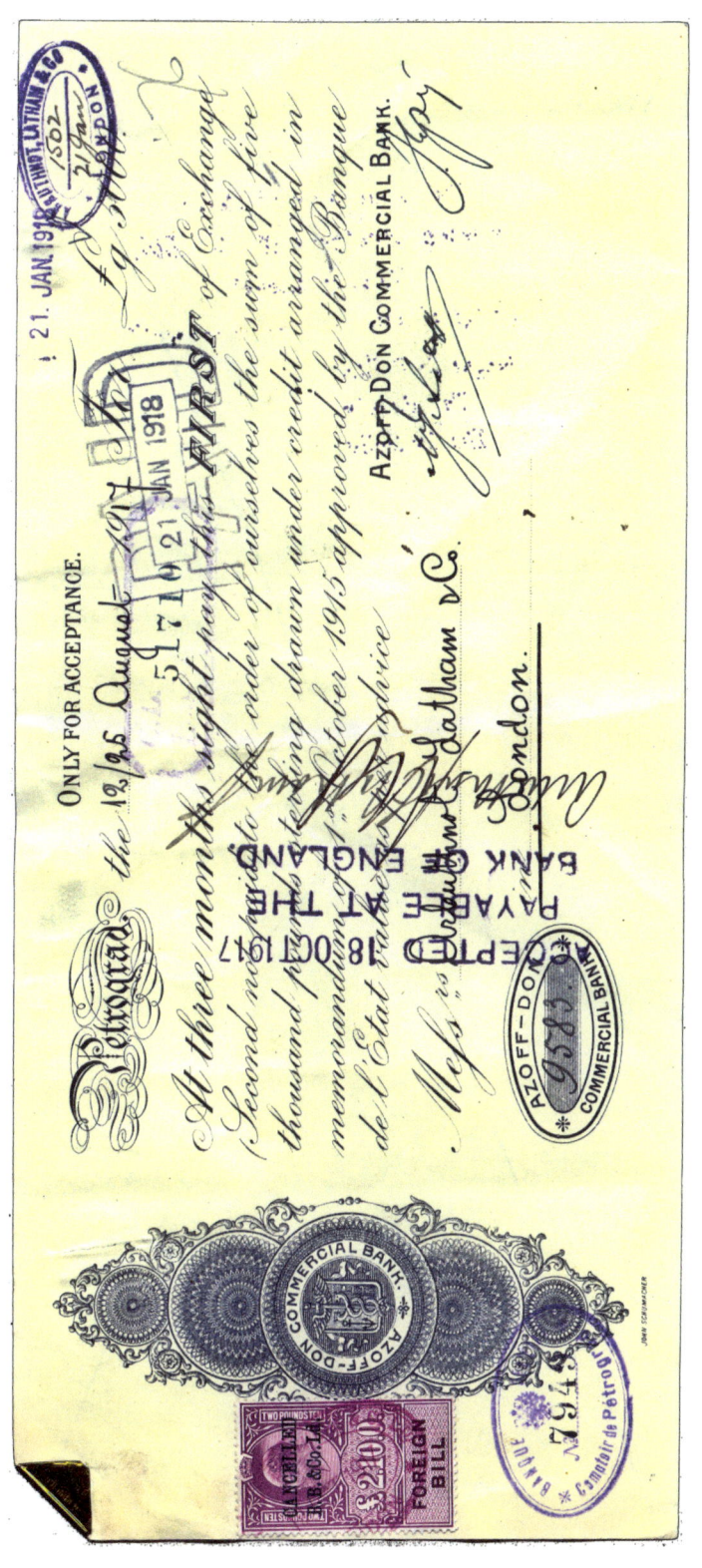

Разрядъ пятый.
200
200
Серія номеръ
9960
Билетъ номеръ
87
ГОСУДАРСТВЕННЫЙ
ВНУТРЕННІЙ 4½% ВЫИГРЫШНЫЙ ЗАЕМЪ 1917 ГОДА,
БИЛЕТЪ
ВЪ ДВѢСТИ РУБЛЕЙ НАРИЦАТЕЛЬНЫХЪ
ПОДДЕЛКА ПРЕСЛЕДУЕТСЯ ЗАКОНОМ
Срокъ послѣдняго купона 16 Мая 1928 года.
AMERICAN BANK NOTE COMPANY.

16 ОКТЯБРЯ 1919 ГОДА
РАЗРЯДЪ ЧЕТВЕРТЫЙ
СЕРІЯ НОМЕРЪ
4 РУБЛЯ 50 КОП.
БИЛЕТЪ НОМЕРЪ 5
Управляющій Государственною Коммиссіею Погашенія Долговъ
Дѣйствителенъ въ теченіе 10 лѣтъ.
3
AMERICAN BANK NOTE CO.

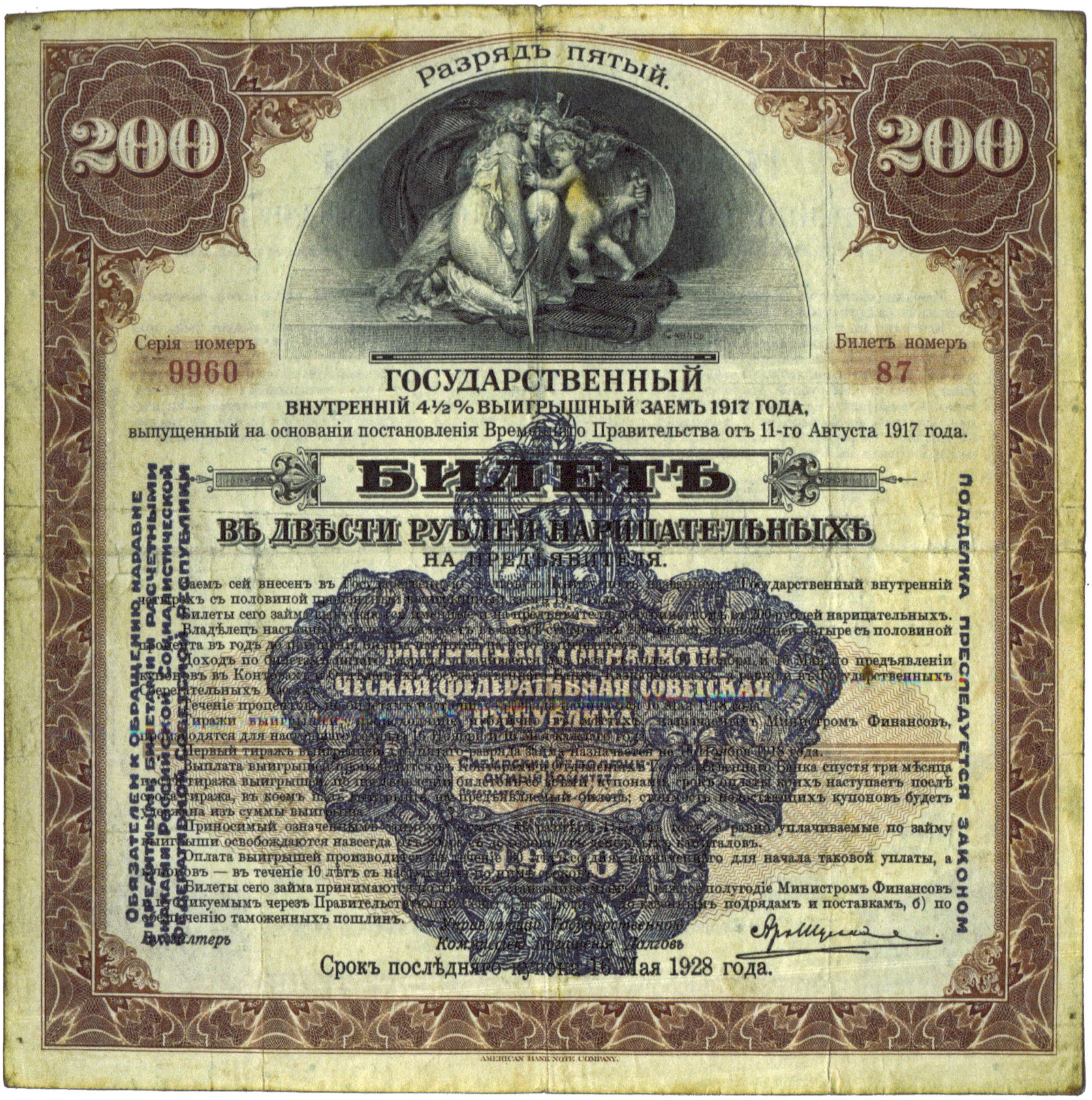

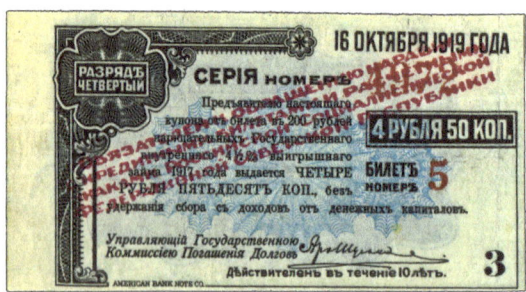

Six: Hyper, Bipaper, and Union

We now return to the story of the Bolsheviks' relationship with their own currency, from where we left it in late 1921 with the rapidly depreciating Sovznaki. While still harboring dreams of abolishing money, the Soviets had begun to acknowledge that, like the World Revolution, this plan would have to be postponed.

Lenin, in particular, hated money and with reason, we must admit. There were all those years in exile—cheap apartments in Finland, Switzerland, and Paris, with peeling paint and patched laundry drying on frayed clotheslines. In 1921, Lenin penned his fantasies of revenge:

> When our victory becomes world-wide, I believe that we will place in the streets of the largest cities in the world public comfort stations made of gold. This would be the most "just" and most educational way of utilising gold…[1]

While entertaining themselves with scatological fantasies, the Bolsheviks continued their pecuniary experiments. In addition to wielding the weapons of depreciation against their class enemies, Soviet planners devised a novel type of paper currency.

Other countries, including the United States, once used a bimetallic standard for money, until they abandoned the idea as unworkable. The Bolsheviks invented the novelty of bipaper, hoping to crush their enemies with one type of paper while using another type for economic planning. But neither depreciation nor bipaper brought the money-free society any closer to fruition, so finally the Soviet Union reformed the ruble and restored a measure of stability.

PURGING ZEROS

Our first example from this period is a massive "Security of the Russian Socialist Federation of Soviet Republics," in the amount of 10 million rubles. This is the largest bill, in physical size and in denomination, ever (yet) deployed in Russia.[2] They were issued only in December 1921, in denominations of one, five, and ten million rubles. These securities made up less than a tenth of the total volume of valid currency, and they are somewhat scarce (admittedly, not rare, since 1.5 trillion rubles were printed in this form). Technically, this is a kind of bond, though no interest is implied—which would have been ridiculous in the face of hyperinflation. It was simply used as another form of token; you can see that this bill was folded repeatedly to fit in a pocket or purse.

Like other forms of money, these securities acquired a pet name. In tribute to their color and perhaps their worth, and as a pun on their denomination, they were known not as *Millioni*, but as *Limoni*, or lemons. There is also a built-in insecurity to these securities, in the fine print on the bottom line. They may be exchanged for accounting tokens until 1 July 1923, but after that date would "not be subject to remuneration." Clearly, something was in the air.

A few weeks after the lemon issue, on New Year's Day, 1922, a new currency appeared with the name of *Denezhni Znak*. Naturally, they were immediately called *Denznaki*. The new bills were still tokens, but "monetary" tokens, *Dengi* being the Russian word for money. The change in nomenclature represents the Bolshevik's first grudging acknowledgement that money wasn't simply going to vanish.

---

[1] Lenin, *Collected Works* (Moscow: Progress Publishers, 1966), 33: 113.

[2] Size reduced by 25%.

Commie Currency

The Denznaki were initially issued in denominations of one to 1000 rubles. The 10-ruble bill shown here has a very low serial number; perhaps it was from the first sheet off the press. The blank area above the serial would show a star watermark if held to the light; curiously, it is not a Soviet star with five points but a Star of David. The reverse explains the most significant aspect of the Denznaki, as shown on this 100-ruble bill from 1922:

> One ruble of the 1922 issue is equal to 10,000 rubles of all patterns issued earlier and acceptance is compulsory at this rate for institutions of the Republic and private individuals.

Ten of these 100-ruble Denznaki equaled one of the ten million Limoni. But even though the Bolsheviks had purged the money's zeros (and they were very fond of purging), they did nothing to solve the underlying cause of the inflation. Quite the contrary:

> The year 1922, however, brought with it such a plethora of paper money that the issue of 1921 was dwarfed by comparison and soon appeared a mere bagatelle. During that year the treasury issued almost two quadrillion rubles, an amount that has sixteen places and that under brighter economic skies is associated with astronomy rather than with finance.[3]

CHERVONETS

When the Denznaki were released into circulation, the Russian price index had passed 138,000. By the end of that horrible year, the index had raced through 21 *million* and finances were becoming truly critical.

Matters would have been even worse if not for the improvements brought about by the New Economic Policy. Food and other products brought to the markets by farmers and NEP-men soaked up a portion of the mass of Denznaki that the government churned out. This was an inescapable fact that must have burned like bile with the Bolsheviks, and perhaps partially explains their repression aimed at those who were keeping the country afloat. It was exactly this time when the GPU, later called the NKVD and KGB, was formed; rule by terror became a bureaucratic function.

It was not simply the ruble's headlong plunge that made finances difficult for Russia's rulers. The quantity of money that could be printed was virtually unlimited, so long as the administration took care to drop some zeros as with the Denznaki. As Lenin pointed out to the Comintern in November 1922, "the noughts can always be crossed out. We have achieved a thing or two in this art…. But what is really important is the problem of stabilizing the ruble."[4]

Yes, it was the unpredictable nature of the inflation rate that made planning, in what was supposed to be a centrally planned economy, nearly impossible. During some months, usually those when private traders brought the most produce to market, prices stabilized. At other times, the index might skyrocket: 40, 60, or 120 percent in just thirty days. Budgets, the

---

[3] Arthur Z. Arnold, *Banks, Credit, and Money in Soviet Russia* (New York: Columbia University Press, 1937), 126.

[4] Lenin, 422.

Six: Hyper, Bipaper, and Union

purchase of materials, and revenue projections became guessing games in this continuing chaos of cash.

Already in November 1921, the Council of People's Commissars had decided that the 1922 budget should be written in terms of pre-war rubles. A series of decrees over the following months dictated that everything from wages to railway rates should be calculated by what was called the *index ruble*. That the Soviets were reduced to planning their finances by reference to the hated empire must also have eaten away at the Bolshevik leaders. But the use of an inflation index for planning purposes, while still using tokens for actual payments, did not solve the government's monetary mess. In late 1922, the Soviets attempted to solve "the problem of stabilizing the ruble" by introducing yet another form of currency.

In the days of Ivan the Terrible (a man much admired by Stalin), the tsar often honored his favorites with decorative medals made from foreign gold coins. Imitations were later produced locally; from 1730, a legal-tender gold coin, the *Chervonets*, was minted. The new Bolshevik bill shared the name and was theoretically backed by three ounces of the gold of its namesake.

Soviet planners meant the exceedingly high-value currency as a stable medium for state enterprises, while the proletariat muddled along with tokens. But a relation between the two components of this bipaper standard had to be announced, if the *Chervontsi* (plural form) were to take the place of the index ruble. At its introduction, a single Chervonets was valued at an astounding 175,000,000 rubles.

Shown here is a modern copy of the first Chervonets, produced for collectors in the 1990s by the Russian Mint.[5] An original is quite rare, as the Bolsheviks printed almost the entire issue in large (compared to the znaki) denominations of five and ten Chervontsi. This was a further attempt to keep them out of the hands of the rabble. The word GOLD appears (in boldface Caps) four times on its face; however, one could not, under any circumstances, exchange the bill for real gold. In a frank retreat from utopian dreams, the new currency was issued by the State Bank, and the words Bank and Banknote are used seven times.

THE AGONY OF THE ZNAKI

To be technically correct, the new banknote was valued at only 17,500 Denznaki upon its introduction. I am describing the progress of Russia's hyperinflation in terms of constant rubles in order to give a true picture of the crisis. At the beginning of 1922, four zeros had been erased from, say, the price of eggs, but twelve months later at least two zeros had been added back.

Merely trimming money did nothing to solve the scourge of price inflation in Russia; the problem can best be understood by reference to the etymology of the word "currency." First used in the 18th century as a name for the medium of exchange, currency was derived from current and ultimately from *cursor*, the Latin for "runner." The function of money is to run or flow through society, facilitating exchanges of goods and services. With the introduction of the Chervontsi, Russian money began to gallop.

When it comes to the pocketbook, people are not fools. Cognizant of the rapid depreciation of their wages, workers hurried to the markets to spend their tokens as quickly as possible.

---

5   This is the only reproduction in this book.

Commie Currency

Traders set their prices in the morning based on their estimate of the token's value at the close of business, then rushed to convert their profits into the more stable Chervontsi or to purchase the commodities they needed. The velocity with which money "runs" within the marketplace can become as debilitating as the sheer volume of bills; this happened in Russia in 1923. As the rate of inflation increased, the Bolsheviks responded by issuing new tokens and cutting off more zeros.

Here are four examples of the 1923 model Denznaki, from the first and second series. The difference is on the reverse, as demonstrated with two otherwise identical 100-ruble notes. On the first, it is explained, "ONE RUBLE of 1923 is the equal of ONE MILLION RUBLES of the Denznaki withdrawn from circulation or 100 RUBLES of the Denznaki of 1922."

By "withdrawn from circulation" is meant those tokens of 1921 and earlier, which were supposed to have been exchanged for Denznaki by January 1923, or July in the case of the Limoni. The second series of new Denznaki, printed after this exchange was completed, states that the tokens should be used in accordance with the decrees of October 1922, when the Chervonets was created.

The first series of 1923 Denznaki was printed in new denominations of up to 250 rubles, while the second ran to 5000 new rubles. Soon afterwards, it was necessary to issue another run of Denznaki; as it turned out, there would be no more.

It is said, "the last shall be first"; curiously, these final Znaki were the first monetary instruments of the newly formed Union of Soviet Socialist Republics. This is a 15,000-ruble example of these last yet first bills, which were also released in 10,000 and 25,000-ruble denominations. The new title of the State is spelled out in the upper right and initialized below the portrait as C.C.C.P.

The new state seal, in the upper left, was adapted from the seal of the Russian Federation on the 25-ruble Denznaki shown above. Marx's motto has been translated into each tongue of the Union's republics (six, at this time), and wrapped as scrolls around the wreaths of grain. The number written in ink, upside-down under the portrait, stands for 565 thousand (a cursive T looks like an M, but with rounded loops). Someone seems to have labeled a bundle of bills with that amount.

To summarize the complicated currency of 1922 and 1923: ten of the 1922 100-ruble tokens equaled one of the 1921 10-million-ruble Securities, while ten of the Limoni were worth just one of the 1923 100-ruble Denznaki. One of the 15,000-ruble Denznaki was worth 1,500 of the 10,000,000-ruble Securities. Finally, by the end of 1923 the Chervonets, having also begun to shrink in value, was worth two 15,000-ruble Denznaki, or 30,000,000,000 in constant rubles.

The peasant who appears as the portrait on this final token seems downcast or tired. Considering the weighty stacks of money that he needed to buy his daily bread, along with the complex scheme of valuation, who could blame him? At the start of 1923, the Russian price index, when compared to 1913, was 21 million. Before the year ended, this index had reached 2 *billion*. The purged 1923 Denznaki, which had begun the year in denominations of 250 rubles and smaller, soon had to be printed in denominations 100 times greater than that. And yet, worse was still to come.

Six: Hyper, Bipaper, and Union

CRISIS AND REFORM

Since taking power, the Bolsheviks had depended on the printing press for much of the necessary revenue for their budgets. Owing to exchange costs and other burdens of hyperinflation, a process of diminishing returns soon set in. In 1918, the new government realized 536 million rubles from the various issues of that seminal year, but in 1922 and 1923 the greatly increased mass of paper only yielded about 300 million per year (in constant rubles).[6] No doubt, the Communists could have continued for some time in this fashion, but the problem of bad paper was forced to resolution by the "scissors crisis."

Both industry and agriculture, the "hammer and sickle," had been damaged greatly during the conflicts of 1914-1920. With the onset of NEP, private farming recovered much faster than did industry, which remained nationalized.

With the introduction of the Chervonets, the government extended large amounts of relatively stable credits to industries, while farmers had to borrow from the volatile private market at much higher rates. Therefore, state industries could afford to withhold products, creating scarcity and driving up demand and subsequently prices. In short, these governmental concerns acted exactly as Marx had accused capitalists of behaving!

One should not be surprised by this. Capitalism, by its nature, tends to provoke competition, demand efficiency and drive prices lower. Socialism, by creating and sheltering bureaucratic monopolies, encourages managers to cheat their customers and insulates them from the consequences of poor economic decisions.

Soviet economists plotted the inflation indices for industrial commodities and agricultural products as separate curves; when placed on the same graph they gave the impression of scissor blades. Hence, economists and political leaders spoke of the "scissors crisis" and "closing the scissor blades." In the villages, those blades were already closing, bearing onto the farmers who found prices for necessaries rising much faster than the sums they could get for their produce. Once again, food became scarce in the cities.

Two opposing proposals were discussed to deal with this problem. One group, headed by economists with a sense of reality, wanted to deal with inflation by balancing the budget, and to encourage industrial competition by reducing domestic credits and importing products.

Trotsky insisted that industry should be built up by increasing credit and further extending central planning, in other words, by emphasizing the very policies that had brought about the crisis. Lenin was out of this fight; his third stroke in March 1923 had reduced him to repeating single syllables such as "vot-vot" (here-here).[7]

In the end, economic reality prevailed, and perhaps that is unfortunate, since otherwise the Soviet government might have fallen. Instead, monetary reform was imposed in March 1924, but not before speculation and inflation became truly frenetic.

---

6 The following explanation of the economic crisis is adapted from Dr. Arnold's fascinating and informative study. My copy was once owned by Alexander Sachs, a Wall Street economist and friend of Albert Einstein. In 1939, Sachs brought Einstein's letter on the nuclear bomb to President Roosevelt. The book also has the library stamp of the Lehman Corporation. Yes, Lehman of the crisis of 2008; I bought the book before they went bust. Perhaps if they had read it…

7 Orlando Figes, *A People's Tragedy*, (New York: Viking, 1997), 801.

Commie Currency

On New Year's Day, 1924, the price index was just under five and a half billion. By the beginning of February, it had passed 16 billion, and in early March 60 billion token rubles were the equal of one Tsarist ruble. On 7 March, the government announced that tokens would be exchanged for new rubles at a rate of fifty billion to one. The index then stabilized; of the token, "it might be said to have lapsed into a coma and expired without regaining consciousness."[8]

At the time of the announcement, the new ruble had already been released into circulation, with its value pegged at ten to one relative to the Chervonets. The volume of the new currency was also a fixed ratio, two new rubles printed for each Chervonets.

This is a bill of the 1924 monetary reform, printed in the attention-getting vertical format. It is marked as "ONE GOLD RUBLE," although it could not be exchanged for gold. Even the background is gold, perhaps to emphasize its desirability and stability. The new bills were called "State Treasury Notes," signaling that the infatuation with tokens, along with the fantasy of abolishing money, had run its course.

---

8   Arnold, 217.

Six: Hyper, Bipaper, and Union

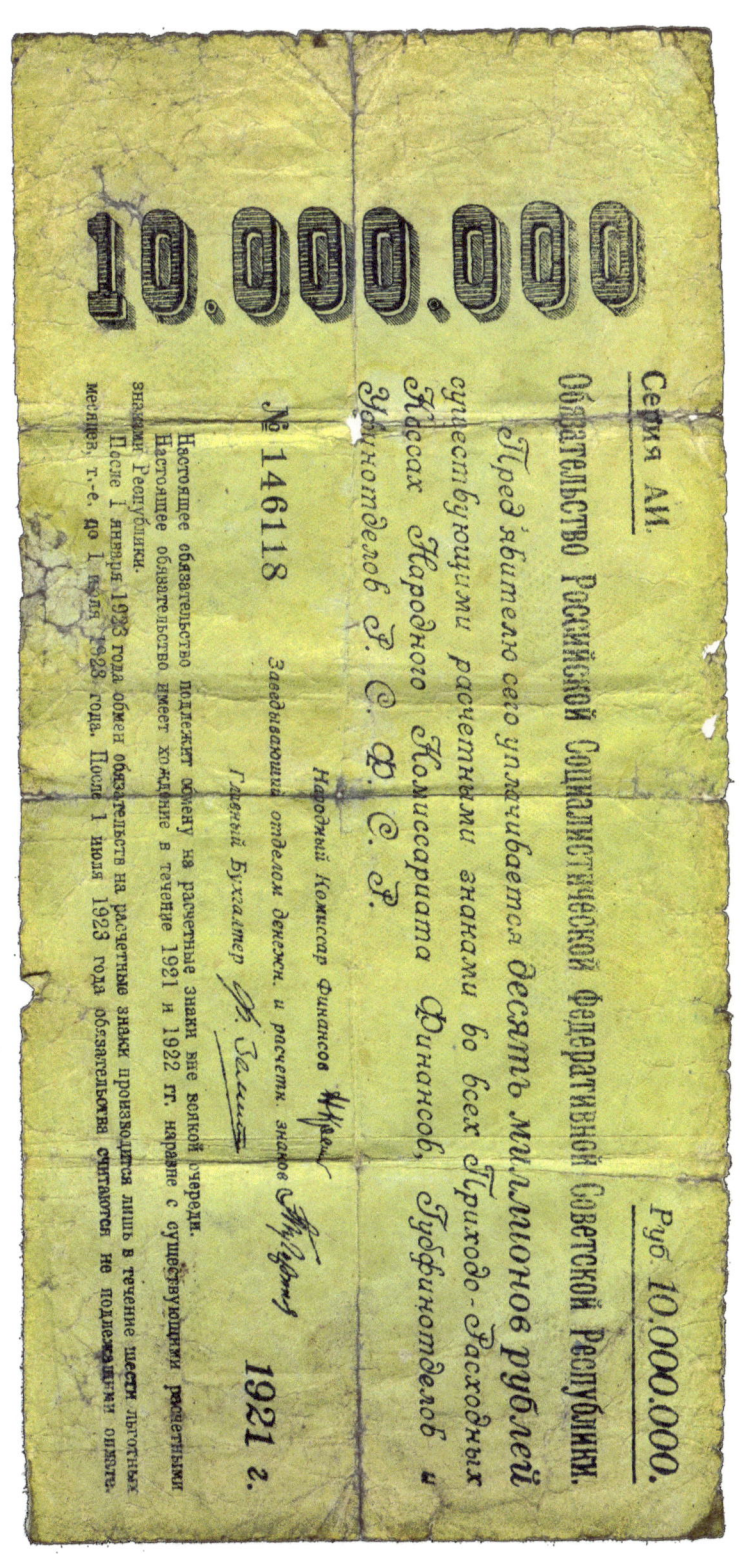

Commie Currency

Six: Hyper, Bipaper, and Union

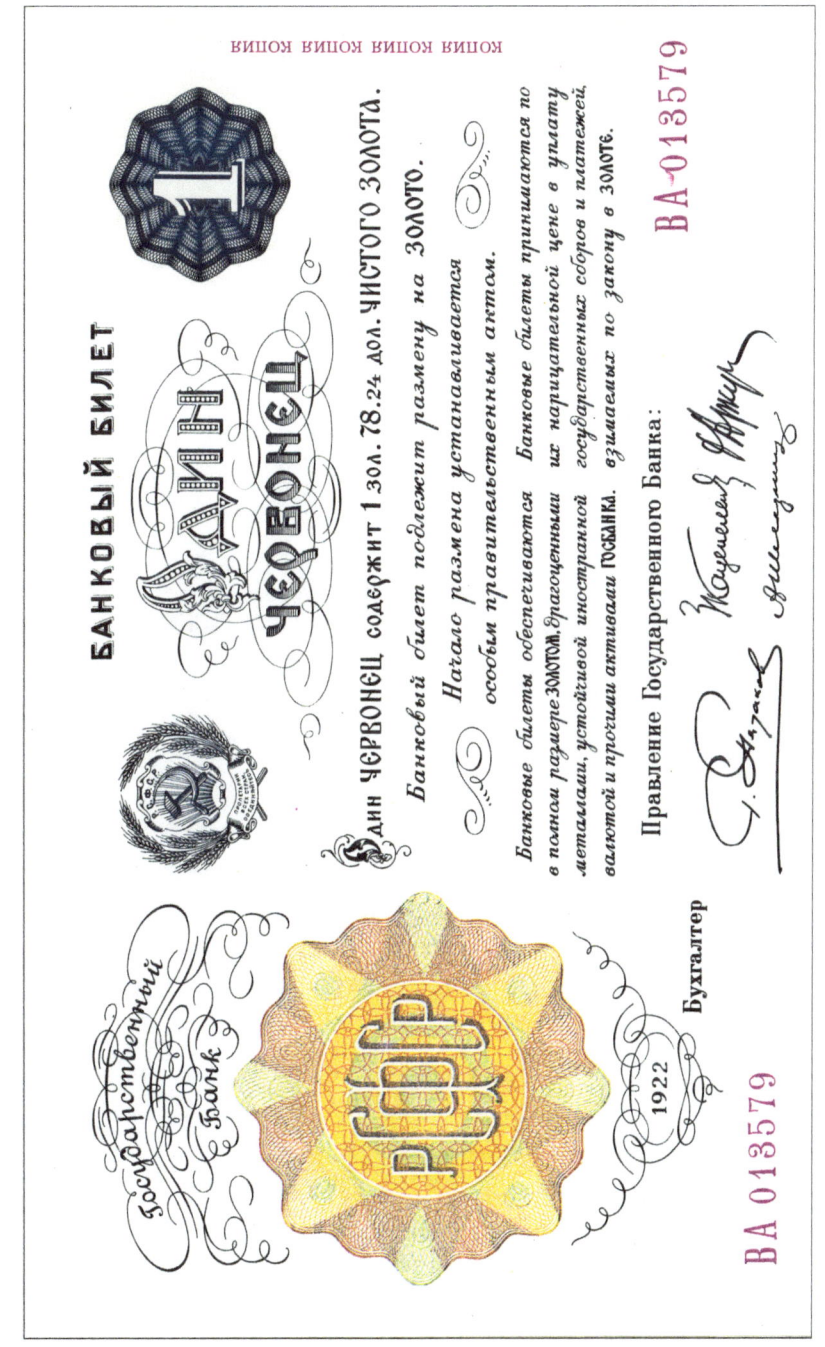

Commie Currency

Six: Hyper, Bipaper, and Union

Commie Currency

Seven: Stability, Suppression, and Stasis

After the reform of 1924, the rulers of the Soviet Union pursued monetary policies that were almost conventional by comparison to the teens and 20s. In fact, the currency became rather boring, with but two major changes, in 1947 and 1961.

This is not to say that the Soviet Union was a place of tranquility. The NEP-men and the peasant farmers were repressed, and replaced by inefficient and inhumane collectivism. In January 1924, Lenin died, and Stalin moved to consolidate the power he had accumulated behind the closed doors of committees. His methodical elimination, of his accomplices as well as his adversaries, climaxed in the Great Terror.

Stalin's double-edged paranoia led him to punish millions who had done no harm, yet trust the one man he could not afford to believe, Adolf Hitler. Nonetheless, Russia prevailed in what they called the Great Patriotic War, despite Stalin's crimes and blunders. Afterwards, Stalin's Iron Curtain set the stage for the half-century long Cold War. Following Stalin's death in 1953, half-hearted attempts at liberalization soon faltered, and the Soviet Union settled into the long Brezhnev Stagnation.

TASTE OF THERMIDOR AND THE QUINQUENNIUM

In the musical *Fiddler on the Roof*, the village rabbi offers up a prayer for Nicholas II: "May God bless and keep the Czar— far away from this place!" The typical peasant only wanted to be left to his *Mir*, a word that means both peace and world, and is applied to the communal arrangements of the village.

In the mid-twenties, the countryside was, to a limited degree, left in peace as a power struggle raged among the Bolsheviks. Under the New Economic Plan, farmers paid a tax in kind and sold their surplus, while "bag-men" brought products of all kinds to city streets.

But Communist purists raged against even a temporary retreat toward a free-market economy. They decried the tactic (for that is all it was) as a Russian "Thermidor," alluding to the month in revolutionary France when moderates suppressed the Jacobins. Ironically, this debate led to the stifling of all dissension.

After Lenin's corpse was placed on display in front of the Kremlin, the question of his successor came to the forefront. In his "Last Testament," the Bolshevik leader had found, not surprisingly, no one to be worthy. Trotsky thought too highly of himself, Bukharin was too much of an egghead, Kamenev and Zinoviev were too squeamish, and Stalin was just plain rude.

Because of his misgivings about Stalin, Lenin recommended that another comrade take his place as General Secretary, but it was already too late for that. The best chance to remove Stalin had been during the Georgian question (chapter four); now *Koba*, as he was known in the inner circle, used the economic debate to discredit his competitors.

Trotsky vehemently opposed NEP, so Stalin portrayed "Trotskyism" as anathema to Leninism. Bukharin enthusiastically supported NEP, so he became a "rightist opportunist." Kamenev and Zinoviev were portrayed as wishy-washy equivocators. Only Stalin sat in the center, as a spider occupies the center of his web, tactically moving Left or Right to consume his victims.

While a life-and-death struggle raged in the Kremlin, the Russian peasant went about his timeless business of sowing and reaping. Money played a relatively small role in this life. Because industry remained firmly in Communist hands,

Commie Currency

the inferior products turned out by non-productive workers under incompetent management weren't worth the high prices demanded for them.

The first year after the monetary reform of 1924, the Soviets printed money only in denominations of three and five rubles. Only the latter had a portrait, of a worker in his cap. He looks worried in this example, and with good reason. Urban wages stood at somewhere between one-half and one-third what they had been under the ancient regime and, unlike the farmers, the workers were losing ground. Stalin's answer was, not to extend NEP-style liberalization to the factories, but to take the failure of central planning to the country.

By 1927, the peasants had largely recovered from the depredations of War Communism, accumulating a surplus worth stealing. Stalin moved against the farmers as he had against his co-politicos, by elevating minor distinctions to crucial categories and turning the resultant groups against each other.

Peasants were classified as *kulaks* (a word meaning fist), as middle peasants, or as poor peasants. The first group was to be repressed, the last raised up, and the middle was, like Baby Bear's soup, just right. We are not speaking here of the difference between Bill Gates and Billy Six-Pack; a kulak might have a larger hut or own two cows instead of one. Collectivization was supposed to eliminate these rural class differences and, in addition, improve efficiency with economies of scale.

But the *Kolkhoz*, or collective farm, was a collective tragedy for the Russian peasant. The well off, or those whose neighbors thought of in that way, were exiled, imprisoned, or executed. The middle peasants were also sometimes repressed as well, since quotas of liquidation had to be met. The poor peasants, that is, the drunkards, loafers and fools, were placed in charge of the collectives, with entirely predictable results.

Famine returned, and was used by Stalin as another tool of repression, mainly against the Ukrainians. (He had complained there were too many of them to send into exile.) "Allowing for famine, violence, hypothermia, and epidemics caused by the disruption, the number of excess deaths between 1930 and 1933 attributable to collectivization lies between a conservative 7.2 and a plausible 10.8 million."[1]

Nor were the workers neglected while the peasants were being brutalized. The production of factory goods was to be greatly increased, along with the building of massive new power plants, dams, mines, etc. A Socialist orgy of expansion was supposed to take place within a period called *Pyatiletki*, the Five-Year Plan.

The first Communist QuinQuennium ran from 1928 to 1933, when, for example, the production of steel was to increase 160% and personal income 506%. This didn't happen. The Second Five Year Plan began even before the first ended, and entertained similar fantasies. A popular slogan of the time said it well: "We will fulfill the Five-Year Plan in four years!"

The government sold bonds (domestically, of course) to help finance the Pyatiletki. This is a 500-ruble bond issued in 1936, the fourth year of the second five-year plan.[2] It bears the signatures of Kalinin, who was the nominal head of state of the USSR, and Molotov, of cocktail fame. This bond was to mature in twenty years, and proclaims in large print, "your money cannot be lost." As we shall see, that was another lie.

---

1 Donald Rayfield, *Stalin and his Hangmen*, (New York: Random House, 2004), 191.
2 Size reduced by 25%.

Seven: Stability, Suppression, and Stasis

Bonds were issued by the State Bank, which the Communists, monopolistic maniacs, envisioned as the sole necessary banking institution in the workers' paradise. The State Bank maintained accounts for all economic entities. These Pyatiletki bonds were a useful way to soak up part of what was being called "the currency overhang," that is, excess money. But they were not necessary since money was created as needed.

> The Five Year Plan was conceived on the basis of a money economy.... [But] the gravest fact was the disappearance of economic calculation.... Once the plans were sanctioned by the government, money for their execution could always be obtained from the bank.[3]

If Lenin Shoe Plant #20 notified the bank that it had delivered 1000 pairs of shoes to Universal Store #37, then the allocated production costs would be automatically credited to the shoe factory and debited from the store's account.

It wouldn't matter if the shoes had all been made to fit the left foot; the plant would still be paid. It did not matter if the store had long since exceeded its credit line; the transfer would be made just the same. It did not matter if the shoes were never sold.

The lack of accountability in production and finances, coupled with the repression of nearly everyone of initiative, ensured the endemic poor quality of available consumer goods. In typically macabre humor, people asked: "What's the difference between a Soviet automobile and a Soviet prison cell? You can close the door on the prison cell."

---

3 Boris Brutzkus, *Economic Planning in Soviet Russia* (New York: Hyperion Press, 1993), 133, 163.

THE GREAT TERRORIST

There is a marked reluctance in some quarters today to use the words "terrorist" and "terrorism." Palliatives such as "insurgent" are instead employed and, in a cliché of relativism, it is claimed, "one man's terrorist is another man's freedom fighter." But like most concepts for which pundits demand a nuanced treatment, terrorism is easily comprehended (and is meant to be). A terrorist is one who hopes to achieve his objectives by producing a panic that paralyzes those who could overwhelm him. The master of this strategy, perhaps the greatest terrorist of all time, was Iosif Dzugashvili, known to his friends as Koba and to history as Stalin, the "Man of Steel."

Stalin played a minor role in the October Revolution; at that time Lenin had trouble remembering his name and often referred to him as the "Georgian." But Koba cunningly laid his path to power, by heading the drudge work committees and finding positions for various monsters who then owed him all. After Lenin's death, Stalin deftly played the Left against the Right, striking in one direction, then the other.

He first killed his adversaries, then his friends, and finally turned his attentions to the masses of completely innocent citizens. As regards the major figures in categories one and two: Trotsky had an ice pick stuck in his head; Kamenev, Zinoviev, and Bukharin were merely shot.

It is the Twenty Million who need to be acknowledged. That is the usual figure now ascribed to the hapless hordes that perished in Stalin's prison camps, though it could easily be double that. Mass graves are still being uncovered. Investigators total up the victims not by counting skulls, which were sometimes left in

Commie Currency

pieces by the executioners' bullets, but by dividing the number of femurs by two.

During the Great Terror, you could be arrested for failing to meet the impossible demands of the Five-Year Plan, for not reporting a friend's injudicious comment, for collecting stamps (foreign contact), or simply to meet a quota. One Soviet joke has a new *zek* telling his cell mates that he was sentenced to ten years "for nothing." "Impossible," he is told, "for nothing you only get five years."

Each case was multiplied by its accomplices, that is, friends and family of the accused. To be the "Wife of an Enemy" was considered a capital offense. Children went to State Orphanages, another form of prison, but after April 1935, those twelve and older became subject to "all measures of criminal punishment."[4] That is, in order to build the Worker's Paradise, grown men executed children—usually in the same way as adults, with "nine grams of justice" in the back of the head.

The implacable and random nature of The Great Terror paralyzed the populace, who lived in a climate of fear impossible for Westerners to comprehend. Every word had to be calculated, every expression guarded. It was said that a man could speak freely only at home and under the blankets. Every night was spent in fear, waiting for the fists on the door.

One common anecdote has a couple quaking in fear when they hear the knock, only to learn in relief that it is just the neighbor, come to tell them that the building is on fire. When the Black Ravens parked outside, and the boots pounded upstairs, no one was safe. Stalin's reign marks the acme of terrorism; Koba stands as a paragon of inhumanity.

For each citizen who was murdered, many more went to the labor camps. Intended to be self-supporting, the camps never turned a profit, but nonetheless formed a significant part of the Soviet economy. Prison camps "were organized around gold mines, coal mines; highway and railway construction; arms factories, chemical factories, metal-processing plants, electricity plants; the building of airports, apartment blocks, sewage systems; the digging of peat, the cutting of trees, and the canning of fish."[5]

Like any other economic venture, the camps required accounting procedures, and had their own money. This is an "Accounting Check" for five rubles, printed in the worst year of the Terror, 1937. The legend at top reads "Central Directorate for the Northern Camps." The initial letters of the first two words, G and U, and the first syllable of the last word, LAG, spell out the acronym by which the whole prison system was known. This term was enshrined in the title of Solzhenitsyn's masterpiece, *The Gulag Archipelago*. (Archipelago has no ending o in Russian, so the two words rhyme.)

The scrip's reverse bears the stamp of the "People's Commissariat of Internal Matters of the USSR" and the phrase "KaMurLag N° 9." This may refer to the region of Karelia, or to the Murmansk Oblast, both located in Northern Russia. Pasteboard vouchers such as these were used by camp administrators as a form of internal petty cash; convicts, of course, were not paid for their labor.

1937 also brought the final issue of one half of the bipaper standard, represented here by a

---

4 Announcement, *Pravda*, in Martin Amis, *Koba the Dread*, (New York: Hyperion Press, 2002), 8.

5 Anne Applebaum, *Gulag*, (New York: Anchor Books, 2004), 217.

Seven: Stability, Suppression, and Stasis

3-Chervonets (they also came in denominations of one, five, and ten). When first issued in 1922, the Chervonets had enjoyed a high premium over the monetary tokens, but later circulated at parity with treasury notes.

In the intervening years, the Chervonets had still served as a standard: it was theoretically backed by gold, and the quantity of treasury notes issued was theoretically limited by the quantity of Chervonets in circulation. In fact, you could never obtain gold for Chervontsi, and after 1928, the limiting ratio to treasury bills was raised repeatedly. In 1937, the Soviets dispensed with this charade, although, as we shall see, a vestige of the bipaper standard remained in subsequent monetary issues.

With the last of the Chervontsi, Lenin makes his first appearance on Russian currency. On this bill, he looks more like a stern schoolteacher than the murderous despot he was. Following the death of Stalin, it became fashionable, among apologists of the Left, to regard Stalinism as an aberration of Leninism. But in the matter of terrorism, at least, Lenin was Koba's mentor.

> On many occasions he [Lenin] stressed that the 'proletarian state' was 'a system of organized violence' against the bourgeoisie: this was what he had always understood by the term 'Dictatorship of the Proletariat'.[6]

Stalin merely expanded the definition of people to which organized violence could be employed. Eventually, the objects of his wrath included almost everyone, with one crucial exception.

---

[6] Orlando Figes, *A People's Tragedy* (New York: Viking, 1997), 525.

PATRIOTIC WAR, PAPER REFORM

In addition to being an evil monster, Stalin was insane. His was a textbook case of *paranoia*: habitual suspicion and hostility; total self-absorption to the point of megalomania; a conspiratorial world-view; and a tightly controlled but murderous rage at the slightest offense. But there was one individual whom Stalin trusted, perhaps because, like Stalin himself, he was an insane and all-powerful dictator. Koba kept his faith in Adolf Hitler against all reason when circumstances screamed otherwise.

Throughout the spring of 1941, from a variety of sources, The All-Wise Leader received notices of the impending Nazi invasion. Stalin rejected each and every report out-of-hand, typically scrawling "provocation!" in the margin. Even after the bombs began to fall in Kiev, the Crimea, and the Baltic States, Koba ordered his forces not to respond to 'provocations.' When Stalin finally grasped the reality of the attack, he collapsed in shock; Molotov had to announce the onset of hostilities to the citizens.

When Molotov and other members of the Politburo then entered Stalin's sanctum in the Kremlin, they found the Glorious Leader huddled in fear and expecting arrest. Certainly, he deserved it. During the Terror, Stalin had purged three of his five marshals, eight of his nine admirals, and some 43,000 lesser officers.

But rather than arrest him, Stalin's followers set him on his feet, dusted him off, and before long the Leader's delusions had properly re-formed and he was able to issue orders. The Russian people eventually won their Great Patriotic War, in spite of Stalin and at a cost of another twenty million lives, or more.

Shortly before signing the short-lived Nazi-Soviet Pact in August 1939, new treasury notes

Commie Currency

were issued, in denominations of one to five. The worker on this one-ruble bill, jackhammer slung casually over his shoulder, is a symbol of the "successes" of the Five Year Plans. If he survived the initial attacks by the Nazis, then he would have been hurriedly evacuated east of the Urals, along with his disassembled factory, to produce armaments.

The five-ruble note has a picture of a pilot, with his aircraft in the background. Russian pilots were as brave and capable as any, but Stalin ordered them to remain on the ground in the opening hours of the war. As a result, more than 1500 planes were destroyed on the tarmac. Moreover, ammunition was in such short supply that some pilots attempted to destroy German aircraft by ramming them.

This pilot is wearing a parachute, but during the war, silk was in such short supply that paratroopers were ordered to jump from low-flying aircraft without them, aiming for snow banks. The experiment did not work well.

Russian civilians endured shortages of basic goods, and rationing continued after the end of hostilities. In addition to meat, eggs, and sugar, such basic foods such as bread and potatoes were restricted. At the same time, there was an abundance of cash. The classic definition of price inflation is "too much money chasing too few goods." Denying that inflation could exist under socialism, the Soviets nevertheless attempted to solve the problem: not by increasing production, but by eliminating part of the money supply.

In early December 1947, stories of panic buying leaked out of the USSR. Many stores closed their doors against crowds eager to exchange rubles for clothing, household goods, anything available.

One report said a peasant woman bought two coats with a bundle of rubles apparently long buried, after difficulties with a store cashier who was loath to accept the money because of its filth and smell."[7]

Waves of frantic spending were sparked by rumors that the government would soon devalue the ruble, rumors denied by Soviet diplomats overseas (they weren't talking in Moscow). On 14 December, the Central Committee announced the pending exchange of all currency, at a cash rate of ten old rubles for each new one. This blow was softened by the end of rationing; some food prices were raised, while others were lowered. Bank savings were exchanged on an equal basis up to 3000 rubles and anything above that at a worse rate. Wages remained the same.

The intent and effect was to confiscate cash from the economy, to punish those who, like the "peasant woman," had set something aside. The American Embassy was among those caught in this trap. They kept large amounts of cash (you have to wonder why) and lost $50,000 in the devaluation, "despite frantic attempts to get rid of it as fast as possible by paying bills."[8] Holders of securities such as our 500-ruble bond could exchange them at a rate of three to one, thus losing two-thirds of their (dare I say it) capital. So much for the guarantee that "you can't lose!"

This draconian technique of controlling inflation by confiscating currency was devised by Deputy Minister of Finance P. Malietin. Two

---

7 "Panic Buying Sweeps Russia, 'Voice of America Reports,'" *New York Times*, 4 Dec. 1947, 14.

8 "U.S. Envoy Out $50,000 In Russian Revaluation," *New York Times*, 20 Dec. 1947, 10.

Seven: Stability, Suppression, and Stasis

years later, he boasted of his accomplishment to US State Department official Paul Nitze:

> I worked out a program under which we one day announced that all ruble currency and all deposits in the banks were declared worthless... suddenly we had no more inflation.[9]

Some of the new currency was printed in the attention-getting vertical format used 23 years previously, such as the one ruble note shown here. More scrolls have been added to the state seal as more Republics were added to the USSR. "One Ruble" is repeated on the bill, once in the language of each Republic. The Baltic States, forcibly annexed in 1940 under the Molotov-Ribbentroff pact, appear on the bottom line.

Denominations of ten rubles and above reverted to a horizontal format, with the bills getting physically larger up to 100 rubles, the highest denomination. Lenin returned to the currency, as shown on this 25-ruble bill; he has changed his tie since 1937. The reverse of this oversize 100-ruble bill[10] features a lovely riverside view of the Kremlin.

The new currency required advanced printing presses, of which the USSR had only one, purchased some time before from the US, with no way to get any more. The solution found was to disassemble this press and copy each part, a technique that the Soviets had used with other American products. The Soviet TU-4 bomber, for example, was a clone of the American B-29 Superfortress.

With their reverse-engineered presses, the new money was as strong as American currency and "somehow resembled the samples of the tsarist currency that could be still remembered by the older generation."[11]

It might be appropriate to ask, four decades after the Revolution, the same question posed in 1913: what was a ruble worth? The average monthly wages ran from 450 to 700 rubles, so these three bills were roughly a week's pay. The *NYT* placed Russian wages against the official prices for various items and found that the average Russian worked half-an-hour for a loaf of bread and nearly eleven hours for a pound of butter. Americans worked 7 minutes for the bread and 48 minutes for the butter.[12] Soviet officials objected that Americans spent one-third of their wages on rent while Soviet citizens paid less than ten percent of their salaries for their apartments (and worth it, to be sure).

The Long Goodbye

The three decades following Stalin's demise were, ironically, the years of the Union's greatest power and prestige overseas, but a time of deepening stagnation and inertia at home. Feeble attempts at reform showed few positive results, and events in the Union's satellite nations shocked Soviet leaders into hibernation. Third-World revolutions generated a degree of Socialist fervor, but the debacle in Afghanistan and the Reagan/Thatcher counter-attack left the hidebound Kremlin reeling. When a reformer

---

9   Paul Nitze, *From Hiroshima to Glasnost: at the Center of Decision: a Memoir* (New York: Grove Weidenfeld, 1989), 74-75.
10   Size reduced by 15%.

11   GOSZNAK Web Site, 26 July 2005.
12   Will Lissner, "Prices In Russia Far Higher Than Ours In Terms Of Work," *New York Times*, 21 December 1947, 1.

Commie Currency

came to power in the mid-eighties, he promised a new era of "rebuilding" and "openness."

The only measure of justice meted out to Stalin in this world was in the manner of his death. Around noon on 1 March 1953, Koba signaled the kitchen staff to make tea. The signal to serve was never received, and such was the fear inspired by the despot that eleven hours passed before any of his staff would investigate.

They found him lying on the floor in soiled nightclothes, fully conscious but unable to speak, having suffered a massive stroke. Koba lingered for four days, and in the end choked to death, his minions watching as his features blackened. The dictator's final gesture was to thrust his hand upward, perhaps in anger or fear of the God he had long ago rejected.

After Stalin was safely placed under glass next to Lenin, a struggle for power wracked the inner circle of the Kremlin. Khrushchev eventually gained preeminence, but the USSR never again invested all power in the hands of any one man. "De-Stalinization" became the nation's passion; Khrushchev hoped to return to Russia's roots, that is, Leninism. The new Premier's attempts at "Reform Communism" were never intended as liberalization; although supposed to be forward-looking, they were inspired by stubborn nostalgia.

Khrushchev used differing methods to stimulate agriculture and industry; neither way worked. With the farms, the new leader enlarged the size of the collectives, in other words, more of the same. Although grain production finally reached 1913 levels, Khrushchev's extravagant claims that he would exceed the US in butter, eggs, and meat proved laughable. In the industrial sector, Khrushchev dispersed many of the central ministries, hoping to encourage local control. However, central planning remained, so in practice this meant that goals and quotas were set out but instructions were lacking.

Khrushchev's domestic policies were failures, but military adventurism brought his end. In the arms race with America, he attempted to gain an edge with nuclear missiles in Cuba. Caught out and threatened with war, Khrushchev was forced to publicly recant and remove the offending weapons. After a decent interval, he was "retired" to a pension and a dacha, but remained alive to write his memoirs.

Incidentally, Stalin had also retired, as he was removed from the mausoleum and buried nearby, under ten feet of concrete. Appropriately, this physical act of de-Stalinization occurred on in the darkness of 31 October 1961—Halloween.

Leonid Brezhnev presided over the Soviet Union for 18 years, and the term most often associated with his reign is "Stagnation." Events in Prague in 1968, when real reformers attempted to build "Communism with a human face," frightened the Kremlin. Moscow clamped down on its impertinent satellites, and a deadening pall settled over the Soviet system.

The Plan was the word, but the world was not only changing, it was changing faster, and the innate deficiencies of the centrally planned economy became more apparent. Another joke told the whole story. It seems there was a train carrying Stalin, Khrushchev, and Brezhnev. When the train broke down, Stalin ordered the crew shot and a new crew brought in. The train began to move, but soon broke down again. This time, Khrushchev pardoned the crew and set them to repairs. The train once more set off, but again ground to a halt. Brezhnev closed the curtains and suggested, "let's pretend we're still moving."

In the Sixties and Seventies, Soviet standing in the world, and perhaps their own

Seven: Stability, Suppression, and Stasis

self-confidence, depended entirely on military victories, most especially in Cuba and Vietnam. This is ironic, considering that Western friends of the USSR generally described themselves as anti-war activists who opposed their own government's use of military power. The US spent about 5% of GDP on the military during this time, including the Vietnam War; for the USSR the figures lay somewhere between 25 and 40%.

America pursued a policy called "Détente" during these years. The idea was that assisting the Soviets economically might encourage them to moderate their political policies. But while in the West politics respond to the economy, in the USSR economic policies were entirely dictated by political concerns. From War Communism to NEP, from Kolkhoz to Sovnarkhoz, every aspect of the Soviet economy was laid down by fiat from above. So, Détente's attempt to influence Soviet leadership by assisting the economy was simply spitting against the wind.

Events in the early Eighties ended the period of stagnation and ushered in a new reformist leader. Soviet military success came to an abrupt end with the debacle in Afghanistan. Newly elected President Reagan, who dared to speak of an "evil empire," proposed an arms race that would be ruinously expensive for the Union. Privatization became popular among several western nations that had formerly edged toward Socialism.

Brezhnev died in 1982, and his successors passed so quickly through the Kremlin (Andropov 15 months, Chernenko just over a year) that a revolving door might have been installed. The uncertainties of the times facilitated the selection of a man of whom Margaret Thatcher said, "the West could do business." The business of Mikhail Gorbachev turned out to be, unwittingly and unwillingly, the dismemberment of Communism.[13]

During the long Time of Stagnation, fittingly, the currency changed only once, in January 1961. For weeks, the citizens had been told that the ruble was going to be improved, to be worth more relative to foreign currency. Just after New Year's Day, the exchange began, at a rate of ten old (1947 type) rubles for each new ruble. Prices, wages, and savings all had a zero struck off.

A litany of reassurances, and a period of three months to exchange old money, meant that no panic buying took place as it had in 1947. But the claim that the government was strengthening the ruble was a transparent lie. The official foreign exchange rate was set at one new ruble for $1.11, but its equivalent of ten old rubles had been valued at $2.50.

Studying Soviet claims of the value of the new "heavy" ruble, the *NYT* compared prices for consumer items in New York and Moscow. Using official exchange rates, they found that bread cost the same, but butter, sugar, and eggs cost, respectively, two, three, and four times as much in the Soviet capital.[14] A 17-inch television cost $120 in New York, but a 15-inch TV cost $277.50 in Moscow.

However, the Soviet sets came with one feature that the American version lacked; they occasionally exploded. This is not a joke; in 1988, *Pravda* reported 180 television fires, resulting in four deaths, in the first three months of the year. When I visited the USSR in 1991, I noticed that the TV in my hotel room was always kept

---

13 For an account of the collapse and Reagan's role in it, see Timothy Buchanan, *Consequences* (Manitou Springs, CO: Eagle Mtn. Press, 2010), 109-186.

14 Harry Schwartz, "New Ruble Can't Match Dollar On Buying Power," *New York Times*, 15 Jan. 1961, 27.

Commie Currency

unplugged. If I left it plugged in, I would find it disconnected again when I returned to the room.

In comparing retail prices for various sundries purchased in New York and Moscow, the *Times* was, in effect, standing Marx on his head. In the Soviet Union, success was measured by the quantity that could be produced, as exemplified by the Stakhonovites—alledgedly superhuman workers who could fabricate many times the norm of a shift. The American newspaper focussed instead on how much the worker could buy with his wages, as indeed the worker might.

The *NYT* had made the same sort of comparisons in 1947, and the technique was used again in 1952, by the "Better Life" travelling show. This exhibition of American lifestyles demonstrated to East German audiences the superiority of capitalism, using a model home with tags attached—tags that carried prices calculated in labor hours.

> This seemingly guileless calculation of purchasing power challenged a tenet of communist faith. Marx had used "labor value" to define capitalist manufacturing and distribution as exploitative…. A century later, MSA [Mutual Security Agency, an offshoot of the Marshall Plan] exhibit planners radically redefined labor value as the amount of work needed to purchase an item rather than produce it. This changed emphasis turned the concept devised by Marx to reveal the abuses of capitalism into a means of measuring it rewards.[15]

---

15   Greg Castillo, *Cold War on the Home Front: the soft Power of Midcentury Design* (Minneapolis, MN: University of Minnesota Press, 2010), 67.

Here are two examples of the "heavy" rubles; denominations of these bills ranged up to 100 rubles, as with the previous issues. This currency was still in use at the time of my first visit; I kept these, illegally, as souvenirs. Incidentally, these are the bills referred to in this book's dedication.

The portrait of Lenin on the 25-ruble note has the appearance of a classical cameo. We might say that during the Time of Stagnation, the image of Lenin was set in stone. There remains a ghost of currency past in the nomenclature used for these bills. The five-ruble is titled "State Treasury Note," but the 25-ruble is a "State Bank Note." These archaic titles reflect the characteristics of the currency during the bipaper period, but which had long since become a distinction without a difference.

Seven: Stability, Suppression, and Stasis

Commie Currency

Seven: Stability, Suppression, and Stasis

Commie Currency

Seven: Stability, Suppression, and Stasis

Commie Currency

Seven: Stability, Suppression, and Stasis

Commie Currency

Seven: Stability, Suppression, and Stasis

Eight: Had a Great Fall

For me, the final chapter in the Soviet story is the most pleasant to relate. I was fortunate to observe history in the making, and those events remain vivid in memory. It is admittedly agreeable to witness your adversaries milling about in disarray, to enjoy them humbly beg for advice, to watch as they haul down their flag and admit defeat. True, your foes may regroup, reinvent themselves, and carry on as if nothing untoward had occurred; still, victory is sweet while it is tasted.

THE REFORMER UNRAVELS THE SYSTEM

Mikhail Gorbachev may be described as both an idealist and a true believer. Coming of age as the USSR was being "de-Stalinized," Gorbachev believed in the socialist system (his senior thesis asserted its superiority over capitalism), but also in its reform. Comrade Gorbachev was mentored by Yuri Andropov, a delicious bit of irony since Andropov was the Kremlin's leading hardliner.

In 1968, for example, Andropov orchestrated the crushing of Prague's attempt at building "Communism with a human face." That same year, Andropov may have engineered a plot to attack Pearl Harbor with a nuclear missile, while throwing blame on Red China. This latter plan failed, fortunately for the human race, when the missile exploded as it was being launched.[1] Andropov was probably also responsible for the failed assassination attempt on Pope John Paul II in 1981.

It was fortunate that Andropov did not last long (fifteen months) at the pinnacle of power in the Kremlin. Moreover, the generational losses of World War II helped ensure that the torch was passed to a much younger man—in the event, Andropov's protégé.

Gorbachev's agenda may be summarized by those two famous Russian terms: *Glasnost*, meaning openness; and *Perestroika*, meaning rebuilding. His intent was that the Soviet Union would undergo needed reforms in an atmosphere of transparency and accountability. Almost immediately, the new leader faced immense economic challenges, stemming from events in the 1970s and 80s.

On the heels of the Arab-Israeli War of 1973, oil prices shot up by 400 percent, and the economies of importing countries sustained a great shock. The free market, in the US and elsewhere, prompted the failure of oil-intensive industries and accelerated the transition to knowledge-based and value-added economies.

In contrast, socialist central planning insulated the Soviet Union's rust belt from financial consequences, while the exploitation of newly discovered oil fields in Siberia provided the wherewithal to keep the sagging economy afloat.

But a decade later, the oil glut destroyed this financial cushion. The USSR now faced the same pressures to re-structure the Rust Belt, but on a much larger scale, with fewer resources. Worst of all, recalcitrant planners in Moscow remained insulated from the consequences of their actions, and clung to methods unchanged since Stalin. Productivity, which had slipped into negative growth sometime in the 1970s, accelerated its decline.

In 1986, the same year that recorded a decline in revenue from Siberian oil, a disaster in Ukraine forced Gorbachev's hand on Glasnost. An ill-planned experiment at Chernobyl's

---

[1] Kenneth Sewell and Clint Richmond, *Red Star Rogue* (New York: Simon & Schuster, 2005), 167, 174-175.

Commie Currency

Number Four Nuclear Reactor resulted in a massive explosion and fire. Soviet authorities reacted in the traditional way, with callous denial. May Day festivities were held as planned in Kiev, and schoolchildren carried red banners through radioactive fallout. Only after the effects were measured in Scandinavia did the Kremlin admit to the disaster. Gorbachev's postulations did little to enhance his credibility, and the episode prompted increasing numbers of Soviet citizens, especially in the provinces, to criticize the regime and consider the alternatives.

Growing cogitation infected the client states of Eastern Europe, culminating in the events of 1989, when those satellites flew free from the Soviet orbit. Because Gorbachev had repudiated the interventionist "Brezhnev Doctrine," he could do little more than watch helplessly as the occupied nations threw off their chains.

Poland was the first to self-liberate, as the once-outlawed Solidarity formed a non-Communist government. Events accelerated when Hungary quit guarding its border with Austria, providing an easy outlet for the prisoners of the Warsaw pact. In the autumn of 1989, I observed the abandoned Trabant automobiles in the Hungarian forests, left where East Germans set out on foot for the West. I spent time in Budapest with a couple from Dresden, who spoke freely of their dissatisfaction with socialism but were at pains to deny any intent to defect.

Soon, that did not matter. The Berlin Wall, when I first visited there in October 1986, seemed an intractable and permanent monument to stupidity. But only three years later, the Wall opened when a mid-level bureaucrat misspoke at a press conference. Berliners wasted no time, and attacked the Wall with sledgehammers; bulldozers took over.

Czechoslovakia also fell away. I visited Prague shortly before the Velvet Revolution, even taking in a performance at the *Magic Lantern*, where the actors soon became plotters and the playwright a president. Everyone, from waiters to policemen, wanted dollars and offered five times the official rate for mine. Flush with cash, I had a pleasant stay in the magical capital of Bohemia. I especially enjoyed the Hradcany Castle; a few weeks later, in obedience to the cries "Havel na Hrad," the newly elected president took office there.

After the USSR lost the colonies in 1989, the Soviet Union itself might have continued indefinitely, and most western analysts believed it would. But in August 1991, an ad-hoc "Emergency Committee," alarmed at the deteriorating economy, and outraged at the proposed Union Treaty (that left out the word *Socialist*), attempted a coup—a maneuver that led to the end of the regime.

As it happened, I arrived in Moscow just one day after the collapse of the coup. I found exuberance in many quarters, but only gloom at *Pravda*, where I spent a day speaking to party journalists.

I was astounded by my reception at the Ministry of Transport, where I had gone to request a visit to Moscow Air Traffic Control Center. I was chauffeured to the Center, given the Grand Tour, and offered an opportunity to fly a MiG; later, the head of Soviet Air Transport, a beribboned marshal, positively begged me to brief him on the structure of aviation in the US. In all seriousness, he listened as I explained how private schools often trained pilots, and described the diversity among air carriers, but he found it hard to believe that airports and other facilities could be privately owned.

Eight: Had a Great Fall

Intourist staff members were likewise perplexed at my presence as an independent traveler. "Where are your vouchers," they wondered, but my dollars, and even my nationality, were trump cards that I used to breeze into fancy restaurants and concert halls.

It is not often that people will admit: yes, we were completely mistaken; you were right and we were wrong; we'll tear this all down and start again. Unfortunately, basking in glory does not last for long, and soon the revisionists found their tongues. Still, I am very glad to have seen for myself the moment, when the statues of Marx and Lenin were toppled.

Speaking of Lenin, the first four bills in this chapter all feature his portrait, though one has been flipped over to show the Savior's Tower. Yes, it was still called the Savior's Tower during the Soviet decades; it was understood that the 'savior' was resting in the glass tomb nearby. Lenin was the *only* person to appear on Soviet currency from 1947 on, but he was no savior, nor were his successors. In fact, the first pair of Lenin bills commemorate yet another dirty trick that the financial masters in Moscow played on the long-suffering Russian people.

Most instances of price inflation result from an over supply of currency, but inflation will also be experienced, even when the growth of money is only moderate, if a severe shortage of goods exists. Productivity had been falling for a very long time throughout the Soviet economy, especially in consumer goods; by 1991, shelves in the state-run stores were almost bare.

However, anything you might desire was available on the black market, which had grown so pervasive that it was referred to, in the government media, as the "second economy." On the street, people called it buying *na levo*, "on the left." In a curious political inversion, stubborn Stalinist types were now called right-wingers, while any hint of the free market was referred to as the left.

Wages were very low, but so were expenses such as lodging. Most workers saved a sizeable portion of their earnings, either to make large purchases on the left, or for their old age. Typically, people did not use state banks, which paid little or nothing in interest; instead citizens kept cash hidden away. Usually, they kept their stash in 50 and 100-ruble bills, the largest denominations printed, like these two examples.

On 22 January 1991, the Kremlin announced that 50 and 100-ruble bills would be "withdrawn" from circulation, effective midnight that day. Soviet citizens were given three days to exchange the now worthless notes, but only in an amount equal to their monthly wages or pensions. Any sum over this pittance could be exchanged only by proving, in some unspecified manner, how the money was legally obtained.

The Government called this extreme measure a blow at the shadow economy, intended to decimate the funds of "speculators" (a communist term for small-scale capitalists). But black-marketeers, or salesmen as we would call them, kept their funds in hard currencies such as dollars or marks. They were relatively unaffected while many ordinary citizens lost their life savings.

The *New York Times* offered its own spin on the Kremlin's confiscatory proclamation. "With hardly anything to buy in the stores here, these vast savings do little more than drive up prices of hard-to-find goods, many of which are illegally pilfered from the legitimate, subsidized state system."[2] The *Times* had certainly changed

---

2 Esther B. Fein, "Soviets Withdrawing 33% of Currency," *New York Times*, 23 Jan. 1991, A3.

Commie Currency

its editorial attitude since they had defended capitalism in 1947 and 1961!

More than a third of the total money supply in the USSR was eliminated, which eased pent-up consumer demands on the flagging Soviet system, but at great cost to the people. The effects were only temporary, however, and before the USSR fell, the State Bank was forced to churn out higher denominations, culminating in the 1000-ruble note shown here. The 500-ruble note next to it was printed in 1992, after the fall of the Party, although the date was relocated to the reverse, as if to hide it from Lenin's gaze. This marks the final appearance of Vladimir Ulyanov (his real name) on Russian currency. Good riddance.

REPEATEDLY BITTEN, FINALLY SHY

After the red hammer-and-sickle was hauled down from the flagpoles of the Kremlin, Russia began the uneven process of joining the capitalist world. A number of crucial errors, some well intentioned and others malicious, increased the sufferings of her people and soured many on the promises of the free market.

In an attempt to promote close trade relations between Russia and the ex-republics of the USSR, Moscow permitted the new nations to continue issuing rubles, in the form of credit. This was done with such enthusiasm that the inflation rate in 1992 was over 2,500 percent.

Russia halted this practice in 1993, and the State Bank announced on 24 July that all currency printed before that year would, after midnight, be withdrawn. Citizens could exchange 35,000 rubles (about $34) for new rubles, but any amount over that would have to be placed in a frozen bank account for six months (where it was soon decimated by inflation).

Once again, the Kremlin had decided to ease its financial woes by confiscating funds from Russian citizens. That cupboard was nearly bare, however, and Moscow was forced to print larger and larger denominations as a new round of inflation raged.

A pair of bills here illustrates this downward spiral. The 100-ruble note, with its prominent tri-color flag, was the smallest issued, and worth less than a tenth of an American cent. Two years later, it was worth only a fifth of that paltry amount, and people hated the sight of them. In 1995, the Russians were more accustomed to paying with the 100,000-ruble note; fittingly, it has the *Bolshoi* Theater on it. Bolshoi is Russian for big, and this was the biggest bill in common usage, worth about $18.

The last pair of bills in this section illustrates the third and final monetary reform, which was the only one that did not cause extra hardships. In August 1997, President Yeltsin announced that, as of the next New Year's Day, three zeroes would be dropped from the ruble.

Having learned from past mistakes, Yeltsin hastened to reassure the public: "Nobody is going to lose anything as a result of the reform."[3] Old rubles could be exchanged for new until 2002, and no savings would be frozen.

The new bills (exactly the same as the old except for fewer zeros) were introduced several months prior to the changeover date of 1 January 1998, which is why the 10-ruble note is dated 1997. For several months, the old and new rubles mixed together in circulation, but the small degree of confusion this might have caused was certainly preferable to the confiscatory 'reforms' of 1947, 1961, 1991 and 1993.

---

3   Stephanie Baker-Said, *St. Petersburg Times*, 11-17 Aug.

Eight: Had a Great Fall

THE PROBLEM OF PRIVATIZATION

"Privatization Checks," such as this example, were intended as compensation for inflationary losses and to provide participation in the shift to a free-market economy. Each citizen received one of these checks in 1992, and was to "invest" it before the end of 1993. By that time, the 10,000-ruble face value represented less than two dollars.

Most people simply sold their checks for cash to agents of the "New Russians," who used them in mass to purchase state assets for pennies on the dollar. These agents stood on street corners, holding placards with their pitiful offers for State assets, stolen decades earlier by the Bolsheviks.

Pictured on the check is the Russian 'White House,' scene of the parliamentary standoff that ended the 1991 coup. After these checks were issued, there was another confrontation at the White House, which ended when Yeltsin's tanks shelled the building and set it afire.

This particular check was issued to Barbara Borzikh, resident of a small town some 400 miles south of Moscow. Born in 1907, she was one of three sisters in a prosperous merchant and land-owning family. Her bright future darkened in 1929, when the Stalinist government demanded the farm and other property. The family resisted, and was literally smoked out when Soviet officials blocked the farmhouse chimney. Miss Borzikh was forced to work for the collective farm, made from her and others' private property. She never married; most eligible men disappeared in Stalin's purges or the Great Patriotic War.

Instead, Barbara helped in those difficult times to raise a niece, Nina, and her children. Miss Borzikh labored for the collective for more than four decades, then retired and received a pension that, thanks to subsequent inflation, soon became worthless. This privatization check was small recompense for a life stolen by a failed social experiment, and Miss Borzikh gave it to her grandniece's American husband, as a souvenir.

But despite the tragedy of her life, Barbara Borzikh remained a happy and devout soul, secure in her belief of a better world to come. When we visited, I admired her strength and cheerfulness—facing adversities that I have never encountered—and I recognized her as an icon of all the Russian babushkas that have kept Russia alive. Barbara Borzikh has since passed on to that better world.

Neighboring Ukraine also issued privatization vouchers, such as this one, although they were called "Certificates." In a curious replay of 1918, the new Rada printed Karbovantsiv (chapter four), in massive quantities. As a result, Ukraine's inflation quickly outpaced Russia's; when the inevitable devaluation arrived, five zeroes were dropped from Ukrainian money, rather than the three in Russia.

The name was also changed, and the *griven* was adopted, or rather, re-adopted. Ukraine's Certificates were valid for much longer than Russia's Checks, until February 1999. When the griven became the national currency in 1996, all certificates were re-valued. You can see the bank stamp above the word "Certificate," with the handwritten amount of 10 griven. But the griven, or hriven as it is often spelled in English, (the Ukrainians are strong on aspiration) continued to decline, from two to a dollar in 1996 to five per dollar when I visited in 2005.

Commie Currency

MMM: A CLASSIC PYRAMID

Soviet citizens were no strangers to financial crime; after all, the government itself was founded on the greatest crimes of the time: nationalization of all land, seizing gold and other assets, repudiation of foreign debts, and so on. Bribery was endemic in the USSR, and it was said that the only way to get anything done was through *blat*, that is, connections.

I once offered 40 dollars to a Soviet bureaucrat to expedite the issuance of an exit visa (for my wife). Sergei Ivanovich was not averse to taking my money, but he bungled the process so badly that his staff delivered the goods before he got paid. He was forced to invent an excuse to see us again so I could pay him.[4]

It has been said that the difference between Capitalism and Communism is that, under Capitalism; man exploits his fellow man, but under Communism; it's the other way around. However familiar Soviets may have been with getting by in a corrupt socialist state, many of them were horribly naïve when an ancient and western confidence scheme appeared in Russia.

In 1994, advertisements in *Izvestia* and *Pravda* extolled the virtues of shares in a new corporation, one that promised returns of ten percent a week. Infomercials on the former state TV depicted ordinary citizens reaping the rewards of vacations in Hawaii, new cars and homes. The corporation spent lavishly from its supposed profits, twice paying for free days on the Moscow subway system. The value of its shares rose each day, and people stood in long lines to invest their savings in this modern marvel of capital.[5]

The reader will immediately realize that this was simply a pyramid scheme, whereby profits are paid to the original investors from the proceeds of subsequent sales, until public confidence is lost and the pyramid collapses. This scam is well known in the West, where it is sometimes disguised as 'multi-level marketing.'

Pyramids, however, were a novelty in Russia, until introduced by Sergei Mavrodi, founder of the MMM corporation.[6] Shares were sold beginning in February 1994, but by July, public confidence was wavering. Rather than retire with his riches, Mavrodi renewed interest in his scheme by issuing fractional shares that looked like, and perhaps were intended to be spent as, money. They even carried the same name as Soviet currency, *biletov*, that is, bills.

MMM was reinvigorated as people again stood in long lines to buy *Mavrodki*, in denominations of one to 1000. The Russian Finance Ministry somewhat belatedly advised the public that the Mavrodki were illegal, and panic set in. Not to be deterred, Sergei Mavrodi issued a second series of biletov, and even ran for the Duma to acquire immunity from prosecution. Eventually, he left Russia and moved to the Dominican Republic.

Here are two Mavrodki, the one-billet and 1000-biletov. They are printed in bright, fluorescent colors and feature portraits of Sergei; on the larger denomination he has been moved to the center. The one-billet is from the first series issued in July 1994. The 1000-biletov is from the

---

4 Naturally, he sent the KGB around to deliver his message.

5 Summary of events adapted from Peter Symes, *MMM Corporation*, pjsymes.com

6 The name is eerily, if unintentionally, reminiscent of M & M Enterprises from *Catch 22*.

Eight: Had a Great Fall

second series, issued in August, and was supposed to be worth upwards of a million and a half rubles, about $250. I paid less than a dollar for it.

It would be easy to smile pityingly at the innocent ex-Soviets, queuing to exchange their hard-earned savings for brightly colored bills resembling Monopoly money. But keep in mind that, at the time, the ruble was shrinking almost as quickly as the Mavrodki was projected to grow. All their lives Russians had secretly known that the West was rich, that they were poor, and in 1991, Russia gave up on her attempt to oppose capitalism. Who can blame the Russians for clutching at the straws of a confidence man?

Eight: Had a Great Fall

Commie Currency

Eight: Had a Great Fall

Commie Currency

Eight: Had a Great Fall

Commie Currency

Eight: Had a Great Fall

Afterword: Money is Information

The history of banking and money in Russia is, in a number of respects, more instructive than that of any other country.[1]

At the dawn of the twentieth century, imperial Russia benefited from a vibrant economy. Like other developing countries, Russia relied on foreign capital investment and the export of commodities. Investment and export were encouraged by Russia's admittedly late development of a modern banking system and by its embrace of the international gold standard. The World War disastrously affected both investment and export, gravely damaging the Russian economy.

The war also freed the tsarist government from the constraints of the gold standard. As expenditures for the conflict rose, the dynasty followed the expediency of printing fiat currency. In this, Russia was not alone. But Russia was unique in that she fell under the control of Marxist radicals, who moved to repudiate private property and began to construct, as Lenin put it, the socialist order.

Marxist dogma states that in the highest stage of socialism, money will be unnecessary since all goods will be produced in abundance and freely distributed. In the transition, however, from capitalism to communism, currency will still have a role to play. The use or rather, the abuse of money in the Soviet Union is the "instructive" narrative.

The Bolsheviks seized power in the midst of a war between nations, and transformed that conflict into a war on private property within their nation. The first salvos in the class conflict were straightforward; in a series of decrees, the Communists seized farms and factories, stores and machinery, homes and businesses. Currency and valuables held in banks also made easy targets. Lenin sent armed soldiers to seize money as needed, and then placed Stalin in charge of nationalizing the banking system.[2]

But even this series of expropriations left a great deal of money in the hands of the loathed bourgeoisie—money that, Lenin said, "represents a claim to levy tribute on the working population."[3] What to do?

In his May 1918 report to the Soviets, Lenin outlined his financial reforms, and warned that the entire Bolshevik platform would be "doomed to failure unless our financial policy is successful." Lenin called for centralizing currency and credit with "a single, strictly defined financial policy." He proposed also a progressive income and property tax—"the only correct tax from the socialist point of view."[4] Finally, Lenin called for the "substitution of new currency for the old." Each person would be required "to declare the amount of money he possesses and obtain new currency for it," and above a certain amount, would receive only a fraction in exchange. Lenin promised that this would be the "last decisive battle with the bourgeoisie."[5]

---

1 Arthur Arnold, Banks, Credit, and Money in Soviet Russia (New York: Columbia University Press, 1937), 507.

2 Ironically, Stalin began his career with the Bolsheviks as a bank robber.

3 V.I. Lenin, "The Immediate Tasks of the Soviet Government," in Collected Works (Moscow: Progress Publishers, 1971), 42:683.

4 In these proposals, Lenin followed, unconsciously, the example of the United States, which had created both the Federal Reserve and the progressive income tax five years earlier.

5 V.I. Lenin, Collected Works (Moscow: Progress Publishers, 1972), 27:383-387.

Commie Currency

The new currency would only be a temporary measure, Lenin declared in his March 1919 draft program for the Communist Party. Lenin noted that it would be "impossible to abolish money at one stroke." Even so, the Party should "strive as speedily as possible to introduce the most radical measures to pave the way for the abolition of money, first and foremost to replace it by savings-bank books, cheques, short-term notes entitling the holders to receive goods from the public stores... etc."[6]

The interim currency, the accounting tokens or znaki, appeared in quantity in early 1920, but mandatory exchange could not be carried out. So long as alternatives existed—this is the first lesson to take from the story of Soviet money—people could choose which currency to use in private exchange. Bowing to the inevitable, the Bolsheviks themselves printed tsarist and provisional money (which circulated at a premium to their designs)—issuing nearly as much, in 1920, as they printed in tokens.

While others dreamed of currencies based on labor or energy, Lenin seems to have been concerned, at that time, only with ensuring that enough money was available. In April 1920, for example, Lenin answered an appeal from Lunacharsky, that teachers in Kazan were "starving through lack of money," with a directive to give preference for new emissions of money to teachers.[7]

Those teachers, and many others, actually were starving, so plans for the post-money millennium would have to be shelved in favor of the urgent problem of feeding the population.

The peasant rebellions, and especially the revolt of the Kronstadt sailors, prompted Lenin to declare the New Economic Policy in 1921. After paying a tax in kind, farmers could sell the rest of their produce on the open market. Almost immediately, the food crisis began to ease.

Rather than abolish money, the Communists strove to print enough to keep up with rising prices; by doing so, they propelled the economy into hyperinflation. Lenin saw this as fitting revenge on the NEP-men who, unlike the Bolsheviks, could feed the Russian people—this is the second lesson.

In his report on NEP, Lenin observed, "you can't call paper currency remuneration."[8] In his 1922 interview with Arthur Ransome, Lenin practically chortled at the naivety of the NEP-men, wondering how it could be profitable that "a small trader sometimes makes millions and millions of profits in depreciated Russian currency, when on the free market a million rubles is worth less that a ruble was before?"[9]

Yet, the deleterious effects of hyperinflation could not be confined to class enemies. By late 1921, Lenin, worried about the "irrelevantly, spontaneously, and irregularly inflated budget," wondered if it was "premature" to form a plan "for restoring our currency."[10] He asked Preobrazhensky if the 1922 tokens, for which four zeros would be struck out, should be made from "bad paper to allow the issued money to be self-liquidated faster?"[11] Sometime in 1921 or

---

6   V.I. Lenin, Collected Works (Moscow: Progress Publishers, 1971), 29:110.

7   V.I. Lenin, Collected Works (Moscow: Progress Publishers, 1975), 44:369.

8   V.I. Lenin, Collected Works (Moscow: Progress Publishers, 1965), 32:290.

9   V.I. Lenin, Collected Works (Moscow: Progress Publishers, 1965), 33:402.

10 V.I. Lenin, Collected Works (Moscow: Progress Publishers, 1976), 45:341-342.

11 V.I. Lenin, 366-367.

Afterword: Money is Information

1922, Lenin realized that the dream of abolishing money was a long way off. The ruble would have to be stabilized, for the sake of the bureaucracies that so dismayed him—but that Stalin loved.

Curiously, the znaki expired at about the same time that Lenin did, in early 1924; Lenin was embalmed and the ruble was stabilized. Stalin, Lenin's replacement, loved stability, often finding it in the grave. He is quoted as remarking that a man may cause a problem, but "no man, no problem."

Stalin had no problem with the continued use of money, calling it "an instrument of bourgeois economy which the Soviet Government has taken into its hands and adapted to the interests of socialism." Talk of abolishing money, he warned, was "leftist, petty-bourgeois prattling… we shall continue to have money for a long time."[12] That settled it; no one wanted to cross Stalin.

And so, Soviet money entered into a long stasis, as stagnant as the economy itself became. Money was created as needed to support the plans; when the supply became excessive, confiscatory 'reforms' solved the problem of what was delicately known as the currency overhang—as in 1947 and 1961. Money served more as a unit of accounting than as a medium of exchange.[13]

Indeed, without the proper papers—residence permit, access to special stores or canteens, vouchers—Soviet money could buy very little. As one former Ukrainian official put it: "A ruble is, in fact, simply a piece of paper which will buy something when accompanied by enough other documents."[14] The Soviet system might have continued indefinitely, but in the 1980s, a reformer took the reins—and there was something very important about money that he did not know.

> Once society abandons free pricing of production goods rational production becomes impossible. Every step that leads away from private ownership of the means of production and the use of money is a step away from rational economic activity.[15]

For Marxists, the above statement is not only anathema; it is nonsensical. They believe that the centrally planned economy is rational; capitalism produces what they call "anarchy of production." In a 1931 primer, a Soviet engineer explained this term with his charming parable of the hats.

It seems, the story goes, there was a certain Mr. Fox who, one day, acquired a million dollars. We are not told where the money originated, just that "it must not remain idle." After consulting friends and reading newspapers, Mr. Fox decides to build a hat factory, because "Hats sell; men get rich." Mr. Box, Mr. Crox, and Mr. Nox also decide to build hat factories and, before long, there are far too many hats on the market.

Suddenly, the public stops buying hats—a development unforeseen by Misters Fox, Box, Crox, and Nox. All their factories go bust and men lose their jobs, but the Foxes, et al, retain

---

12 J. Stalin, "Report of the XVII Congress of the All-Union Communist Party," in Arnold, 446.

13 Peter Rutland, The Myth of the Plan (La Salle, IL: Open Court, 1985), 126.

14 J. Fischer, in Rutland, 140.

15 Ludwig von Mises, Socialism, trans. J. Kahane (Indianapolis, IN: Liberty Fund, 1981), 102. Emphasis added.

Commie Currency

the profits extracted from the now unwanted workers.

After a year or two, the stores run short of hats, and the cycle begins again: with Misters Doodle, Boodle, Foodle, and Noodle. "The experience with hats is repeated with shoes, with sugar, with pig iron, with coal, with kerosene. Factories are blown up like soap bubbles and burst. One would think that people had lost their minds."[16] Such was the perceived anarchy of capitalist production.

Note the very limited role played by money in this story. It appears somehow, as if manna from heaven, and is rather arbitrarily turned into the capital of a hat factory. Thereafter, hat production multiplies wildly until brought to an unexpected halt. Finally, the money drawn from the surplus value generated by labor is transformed again into capital—another hat factory, perhaps.

The parable of the hats is, to be sure, ludicrous. In reality, entrepreneurs meticulously analyze and attempt to anticipate the desires of the consumer. They carefully calculate the costs of myriad materials and means to produce and distribute their products. They receive continuous feedback on the efficacy of their methods and the reception of their goods by consumers. The basic component common to all these calculations is, of course, money.

In the market, the price of anything is determined by the negotiation of the parties making an exchange. As a result, commodities are used in the most cost effective ways—shovels are made from steel, while titanium is used in desalination plants and for propellers (being highly resistant to seawater).

In the socialist economy, prices cannot be set by the market; there is no negotiation because the state owns everything. As long ago as 1920, von Mises demonstrated that destruction of the market would leave no way to rationally (that is, non-arbitrarily) way to calculate relative costs. Ah, said the Marxists, since labor is the source of exchange-value, and exchange-value is only expressed in money, we will calculate costs using socially necessary labor time.

Crucial to this idea is the proposition that labor is homogeneous. "Skilled labour counts only as simple labour intensified, or rather, as multiplied simple labour, a given quantity of skilled being considered equal to a greater quantity of simple labour."[17] The reduction of all forms of labor involved in producing one unit of output to a common denominator gives us, Marx says, the socially necessary labor time to produce that unit, and hence its value.

It is true that the exchange of commodities may reveal that the exchange-value of, say, a machinist is five times that of the person who sweeps up the shavings. But, von Mises points out, "This process of equating is a result of the working of the market, not its presupposition." The attempt to calculate costs based on the relative values of labor, without reference to the market process that determines those values, is necessarily arbitrary—"useless as an instrument for the economic organization of resources."[18]

Soviet planners could and did set prices arbitrarily, largely from inertia—"the system was reviewed in 1967, but had to wait until 1982 for

---

16   M. Ilin, New Russia's Primer: The Story of the Five-Year Plan, trans. George S. Counts (New York: Houghton Mifflin Company, 1931), 6-9.

17   Karl Marx, Capital, vol. I, The Process of Capitalist Production, trans. Samuel Moore and Edward Aveling (New York: International Publishers, 1967), 44.

18   von Mises, 116.

Afterword: Money is Information

its next reform."[19] Also, they cheated, that is, they examined prices in non-socialist economies for clues on price structures. But their total ignorance of cost accounting severely hampered productivity, as we shall see. There is, moreover, another problem with using labor as the source of value.

Suppose the labor time for producing one unit of commodity P, or one unit of Q, is ten hours. Each process also requires material input, A, which itself takes one hour to process. P requires two units of A and eight hours of labor, while Q requires one unit of A and nine hours of labor. P and Q are equivalent in exchange-value, yet P requires twice as much material—coal, oil, iron, or what have you.[20]

Labor value as a means of calculating costs only works if you assume that raw materials have no intrinsic value, which Marx does, airily declaring they are "furnished by Nature without the help of man."[21] And so it was in the Soviet Union, where materials were wasted on a prodigious scale. One industry illustrates both of these flaws in the labor theory of value.

The export of oil and natural gas was the Soviet Union's most important source of foreign revenue. Yet, the Soviets consistently bungled their handling of this vital resource. One Canadian geophysicist reported how drilling in Siberian permafrost was carried out:

> When completing those wells, they did not bother to insulate the well casings. As a result, when the hot gases began to flow up from the reservoir, they melted the permafrost, creating an annular leak around the pipe. A trillion cubic feet of gas escaped.[22]

Marxist dogma dictated this waste, for it would have required additional labor, which had value, to prevent the loss of natural gas, which had none, being "furnished by Nature." Even more costly to the Soviet industry was their unfamiliarity with reservoir engineering, which followed from Marxist ignorance of market relations.

Oil, like labor, is not homogeneous, and is found trapped in diverse formations underground. With each field, market-aware geophysicists construct and continue to revise models that permit extraction at the most cost-effective rates. Running wells wide-open can leave unrecoverable oil behind, while overly choking well production may produce more oil, but at unacceptably higher costs. These techniques were unknown to the Soviets. They simply applied a standard drilling template and, if oil was found, ran the well at full bore to exhaustion.

> There was no place in communist doctrine for the "time value of money." Thus the Soviets had no idea how to calculate discounted cash flows. They had no conceptual tools with which to optimize their production plans.... The damage to the reservoirs was irreparable.[23]

The Soviets earned 100 billion dollars or more a year from oil, cash that was greatly needed to import grain and other necessities. But in the first half of the 1980s, the price of crude collapsed. A

---

19   Rutland, 127.
20   von Mises, 115.
21   Marx, 43.
22   In Thomas C. Reed, *At the Abyss: An Insider's History of the Cold War* (New York: Ballantine Books, 2004), 217.
23   Reed, 218-219.

Commie Currency

good argument may be made that this decline in revenue prompted Gorbachev's reform efforts. Perestroika, however, was doomed by Soviet ignorance of money relations.

Money is more than a medium of exchange; it relays particulars about the most effective ways to use scarce resources to satisfy human wants. Money is information, and Gorbachev did not know that, even as he attempted to impose monetary reforms on Russia.

> Today we are going to examine one of the cardinal questions of restructuring [perestroika]. I am talking… about qualitative changes in the system of the economic mechanism…. A radical reform of price formation is a very important component…. Without this, a complete changeover to the new mechanism is impossible…. What is involved here is not only the level of prices but also *the procedure for setting them*.[24]

Gorbachev understood, because his economists all told him, that the price structure worked out by Moscow's planners was unrealistic. "Our prices for fuel and for mineral and agricultural raw materials are radically understated, while those for machinery are unduly high. They are unjustifiably low for food, housing and public services and unduly high for consumer durables."[25]

The planners' price schedules followed Marxist doctrine. Raw materials were considered gifts from Nature and valued accordingly low. Prices for finished products were set high to make industries seem profitable, after the fact, and after their targets were met. Food and other 'inputs' for labor were subsidized, in order to lower labor costs, the only costs that really mattered.

Gorbachev knew that prices were out of whack, but failed to grasp that they could not be fixed by tinkering with the system of "setting them." Yet, this is exactly what he proposed in 1987. "All of the money that the state is paying in the form of subsidies today will be fully returned to the population in the form of compensation."[26] He believed that prices and wages could be raised simultaneously and in parallel, in zero-sum directives. Of course, this did not, and could not, work.

It is simple, really. An individual perceives his, or her, needs in order of importance and uses resources to satisfy needs in this order. The individual uses exchange to acquire resources. All resources are scarce, to one degree or another, and in the market, individuals bid on these resources. Therefore, market exchange efficiently allocates resources according to human needs, as they perceive them. Money, as the medium of exchange, provides data on efficient resource use. Any interference with the market degrades the quality of this information. As von Mises showed, the market is the only way to calculate the proper ways of using scarce resources.[27]

---

24 M. Gorbachev, "On the Party's Tasks in the Fundamental Restructuring of Economic Management," report to the Central Committee of the CPSU, 25 June 1987, in *The USSR Today: perspectives from the soviet press*, Seventh Edition (Columbus, OH: The Current Digest of the Soviet Press, 1988), 10,14. Emphasis added.

25 Nikolai Shmelev, "Advances and Debts," *Novy Mir*, June 1987, in *The USSR Today*, 4.

---

26 Gorbachev, 21.

27 One might argue that individuals do not correctly perceive their needs; some other entity should make these decisions. But this is social engineering, not economics, and contributes nothing to economic calculation.

Afterword: Money is Information

What happened in Gorbachev's Russia was this. Wages rose, but not productivity; in 1990, for example, income rose nearly fifteen percent, but productivity dropped by three percent.[28] This hardly put more products on the shelves. Consumer prices continued to be subsidized by an administration fearful of what the market might do, and the resultant shortages were exacerbated by hoarding. Sometimes, even salt disappeared. Products were available through the "second economy," the latest phrase for the free market, but at much greater prices. A joke told it all:

> A customer at the private market complained that potatoes cost several rubles a kilo there, but sold for only forty kopecks in the state store. So the vendor asked, "Do they have any potatoes in the state store?" "Well, no." "Ah, you see, I could also sell potatoes for forty kopecks, if I didn't have any!"

When retail schedules were finally revised in April 1991, the prices for food and other consumer goods doubled, provoking "public animosity" and civil unrest.[29] Economic instability was one of the primary motivators behind the attempted coup four months later. In their "Appeal to the Soviet People," the GKChP decried the "sharp drop in the living standards of the overwhelming majority of the population… a flowering of speculation and of the shadow economy."[30]

Members of the "Gang of Eight" were no fans of the market, but the Russian leader who successfully faced them down (from atop a tank) was committed to it. Shortly after the coup, Boris Yeltsin, the first elected president, said Russia is "striving for further democracy, a market economy, and all forms of property, including private property."[31] The Communist Party was outlawed. Gorbachev was locked out of his office in the Kremlin and given a few minutes, on Christmas Day, to resign and dissolve the Soviet Union. The Marxist experiment was over.

> In the market economy the consumers are supreme…. The market is a democracy in which every penny gives a right to vote.[32]

In his massive, and conclusive, refutation of the economic, cultural, social, and political arguments for socialism, von Mises did not reserve his condemnation only for the Bolsheviks. He denounced all practitioners of socialism, including interventionists:

> What the interventionist aims at is the substitution of police pressure for the choice of the consumer. All this talk: the state should do this or do that, ultimately means: the police should force consumers to behave otherwise than they would behave spontaneously. In such proposals as:

---

28 William Moskoff, *Hard Times: Impoverishment and Protest in the Perestroika Years* (New York: M.E. Sharpe, 1993), 90.

29 Moskoff, 102-104.

30 John B. Dunlop, *The Rise of Russia and the Fall of the Soviet Empire* (Princeton, NJ: Princeton University Press, 1993), 194-197.

31 Russian Television, 7 September 1991, in Dunlop, 282.

32 von Mises, 490.

Commie Currency

let *us* raise farm prices, let *us* raise wage rates, let *us* lower profits, let *us* curtail the salaries of executives, the *us* ultimately refers to the police. Yet the authors of these projects protest that they are planning for freedom and industrial democracy.[33]

This is the final lesson. Every intervention in the market, no matter how well intentioned, degrades the efficiency of market relations and has deleterious effects on the economy. Minimum wage laws raise the unemployment rate; price controls create shortages; subsidies distort the allocation of resources, and so on.

But perhaps no intervention is more pervasive and pernicious than the manipulation of the money supply. For if money is information, then banking intervention distorts those signals and inspires misinformed decision-making.

Let us return to the parable of the hats, in which we find a grain of truth. The money in the tale was acquired from somewhere, and this cash powered a hat bubble. In America, money is provided by the Federal Reserve Bank, and the Fed is free to expand or contract the money supply whenever, and to whatever degree, the central bankers desire.

The Fed expands the money supply by purchasing government debt, paying for these with newly created Federal Reserve Notes (commonly called dollars), and placing those funds into the reserve accounts of member banks. Those banks may loan the majority of that money, which in turn is loaned again and again, until limited by reserve requirements. In this way, one trillion newly created dollars may expand to ten trillion or more.

A policy of monetary expansion, sometimes called easy money or loose money (after the slot machine term), is the force that powers economic bubbles. Not hats, of course. Easy money from the Fed powered the recently collapsed housing bubble and the preceding tech-stock bubble.

However, this concludes our history of Soviet money. The story of abuse of American money will be told in the author's forthcoming book: *The Rise and Fall of the US Dollar*.

---

[33] Ludwig von Mises, 491.

Afterword: Money is Information

ABOUT THE AUTHOR

Timothy E. Buchanan has a B.A. in Russian Language and Culture, and a M.A. in History. He is the owner and curator of The Museum of Orthodoxy, which displays artifacts from the Byzantine and Russian Empires, as well as from modern Russia.

His great interest in history was sparked by extensive travel throughout Europe in the 1980s, travel made possible by his first career as an air traffic controller. He witnessed the decline of communism in Eastern Europe in 1989, and was in Moscow in 1991 where, among other momentous events, he met his future wife.

Today, he lives with wife and two children in a low-impact home that he designed and built, in the mountains of Colorado. He is planning a book about this solar-powered residence, *Building Millennial House.* He is also the author of *Consequences,* a set of essays on the effects of the ideology of socialism.

www.ingramcontent.com/pod-product-compliance
Lightning Source LLC
Chambersburg PA
CBHW041510220426
43661CB00047B/1524